Frozen Air

# Frozen Air

Andrew Ray

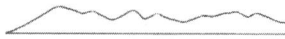

Plinius Press

2017

First printing: 2017

ISBN: 978-1-9998072-0-7

Published by the Plinius Press in London

Vanguard Way
Hope Gap
Coastguard Cottages

Cuckmere Haven

Haven Brow
Short Brow
Rough Brow
Brass Point
Flat Hill
Baily's Hill
Went Hill

Birling Gap

Belle Tout

# Frozen Air

# At the Edge

A few feet beyond me the land ends. The cliff edge is obscured by a low barrier of tangled brown thistles. Behind me the coastal path has been worn into the low turf. To the west it follows the curve of the cliffs and rises gently towards Seaford Head. To the east it will take me to Hope Gap and then down to the river mouth at Cuckmere Haven.

There is another path though, leading straight towards the sea. It is a narrow parting of the long grass, heading away from me, further than it would be safe to walk. Looking in that direction, following its line out into space and towards the horizon, I almost miss a slight movement at the end of the trail. There is nothing more for a minute or two and then the tips of long ears are briefly visible. The rabbit must be right on the brink, where plants no longer have any purchase in the dry, crumbling soil. Waiting for it to return, I wonder what draws it to the edge.

Out to sea there are just a few white sails barely moving. The sky too has no more than a scattering of clouds. The day is warming up but there is a strong wind here, bending the grass and shaking the thistle heads where the rabbit disappeared.

I step back and turn to walk along the track that leads towards Cuckmere Haven. Beyond it are the Seven Sisters, their famous profile already visible where the land before me starts to dip. A little way further along the path and they are fully revealed, a sheer chalk wall where the Downs suddenly come upon the sea.

# Distant Blue

There was a time before I had ever seen the sea. Then, one day, there it was, a distant triangle of blue glimpsed between two hills from the back of my parents' car. It has been said that the most intense aesthetic experiences of nature are those that catch us by surprise.[1] This moment was too long ago for me to remember now just how it felt. I am told that when we turned another bend on the road to the coast, temporarily obscuring the view, I burst into tears, thinking we were leaving the sea behind before we had even reached it.

Later, living in Brighton, the sea was a mostly unregarded presence in the background. If I did go down to the front, I was usually disappointed. The faded hotels, amusement arcades and novelty shops just intensified a sea longing that centred on something much more vast and elemental. Maybe I caught sight of this ideal sea from the top of the Downs or on a walk to the Seven Sisters. It seemed then, though, as if it could only be reached in the imagination. I remember particularly reading one story of a traveller who, after a long journey, climbed a slope and came unexpectedly to the brink of the land. Looking down from the cliff he realised he was in the presence of the Great Sea. Standing there with arms outstretched, he watched the sun set and experienced a profound yearning.[2]

Today, on this path, I can still sense something of what I felt when words like these opened out new imaginative vistas. We tend to feel we must appreciate a place for what it is, rather than filter it through what we have read in books. But every experience is coloured by memory, whether or not the events actually happened to us. Childhood walks were enriched by what filled our imaginations at the time. This is one reason we return to places we have visited so often, so that those old emotions can be felt across the stretch of years, suddenly and briefly overwhelming us again.

# Oceanic Feeling

On the path towards Hope Gap the sea is temporarily obscured by the angle of the ground. You can imagine walking all day and ascending a slope like this, only to arrive abruptly at the edge of England. In the earliest of Western literature's sudden encounters with the sea, Xenophon's *Anabasis*, ten thousand Greek soldiers, trapped in hostile Persian territory, arrive at Mount Theches after a five day march. Those at the rear, like Xenophon, hear a great shout and assume that the vanguard is under attack. They quickly realise however that the soldiers are passing back the joyful news, "Thalatta! Thalatta!" – "The Sea! The Sea!" Realising they have made it at last to within sight of the coast, the soldiers stand and embrace each other.[3]

No doubt the sight of the sea here would be more moving after completing some arduous ordeal, with its blue-grey surface suggesting repose and refreshment. I can picture competitors in the annual London to Brighton cycle ride cresting the final slope of the Downs and gasping "The Sea! The Sea!" Here at the cliffs, this grassy path offers an easy walk. It is called the Vanguard Way and sounds as if it had some heroic history, but the name is relatively recent and honours a ramblers club who acquired their title from having to travel back to London in a guard's van.

For the Greek army, whose soldiers had set out from their islands in the Aegean, the sea was a symbol of home. For those of us who have lived within reach of the sea, the sudden sight of it prompts a surge of memory. But the oceanic feeling, a deep emotional response to the idea of the sea, is more universal. Freud thought it was a kind of return to the earliest phase of childhood, before awareness grows that we are individuals and there are other people in this world. This is why, I think, it is possible to feel a sense of peace up here, even as you stand alone at the furthermost point of the land.

# Pristine Sea

As I walk, I look out over the sea. Sometimes there is nothing there but a consoling emptiness. In his first book, *Pleasures and Days*, a young Marcel Proust described something pristine: 'unlike the earth, the sea does not bear the traces of human works and human life. Nothing remains on the sea, nothing passes there except in flight, and how quickly the wake of a ship disappears! Hence the sea's great purity, which earthly things do not have.'[4]

However, Proust seems to have regarded a longing for the timeless open sea as something one grows out of. The narrator of *In Search of Lost Time*, looking at the English Channel from the French coast, ceases to see the sea as an inaccessible, eternal Ocean. 'There were days now when, on the contrary, the sea itself seemed almost rural.'[5] The sunlight on the water was like a dusty white track and the distant mast of a fishing boat resembled a village steeple. The alternation of sharply defined patches of colour, 'the rough, yellow, almost muddy irregularities of the marine surface, the banks, the slopes that hid from sight a vessel upon which a crew of nimble sailors seemed to be reaping a harvest, all this upon stormy days made the ocean a thing as varied, as solid, as broken, as populous, as civilised as the earth.'

Reading this description you feel the absence now of those people that for centuries worked along the shore on land and sea.[6] These coastal waters will continue to be treated as a resource but its workers will be gone. Engineers at Rolls Royce are developing vast, remote controlled cargo vessels.[7] Here there are plans for an offshore wind farm that will look like a distant grey fence. But for now, it remains possible to look out from the cliffs and entertain the illusion that the sea has a kind of absolute purity, distinct from the land[8]. There are passages of time when no ships cross your field of vision, when nothing but light and water lie in front of you.

# Horizon

From the cliffs you can watch the motion of the waves below as they throw off sparks of sunlight. Further out, there are shifting patches of water that are only as stable as the cloud formations above them. Beyond is the offing, that region of the sea that is distant but visible, a thin band of flint grey. And then a paler region right at the horizon, almost impossible to distinguish from the sky.

Walking this path you are always conscious of a sharp edge to the land. But there is no edge to the world and the horizon as such does not exist, it is simply the point at which our powers of perception fail us.[9] Beyond the horizon the sea continues until it eventually meets the sands of France, its waves breaking on the beach that Proust recollected in his novel.[10]

It was in France, while Proust was working on his book, that a colour called 'horizon blue' was invented. This was the shade of a new uniform, supplied to French soldiers fighting in the First World War. The red trousers it replaced had made them potentially conspicuous to the enemy. Dressed in the indistinct colour of the horizon they would, it was thought, be more elusive.[11]

What is it we look for in the horizon? According to one recent study, it 'beckons towards transcendence but does not fulfil it.'[12] The cliff walk takes us to the brink of the land from where the sea appears boundless. There are no limits on what we can imagine beyond that invisible line. But our sense of wonder has an undertow of sadness at the impossibility of seeing further. Our vision clouds only a few miles out to sea.

# Beyond the Frame

In places the cliff seems almost to hang out over the sea. I stop at a point where no plants cling to the edge of the land. There is only bare chalk, and then nothing but air.

I have walked coastal paths where dense trees hide the view and all you can do is listen to the waves until there is a gap in the vegetation. On the Seven Sisters there are no trees, no fences, nothing to constrain the eye. There are no natural frames on the cliffs or at the mouth of the river. You could duck inside one of the old World War Two pillboxes and look through its letter-box shaped opening, but all it is possible to see from them is a ridge of stones and a strip of sky.

Maybe it is only residents of the Coastguard Cottages here, with their windows on the sea, who think of the view as cropped and composed. They can enjoy a changing series of private seascapes, like the narrator of Proust's *In Search of Lost Time*, who could sit in comfort in his hotel room and look each day on a new view of the Normandy coast, framed in the iron uprights of his window. The sea is less threatening as a pattern on glass.

A frame flattens the world and makes even the sky seem solid and tangible. Walking here, high above the sea, everything seems uncontained. On the clifftops it seems possible to shake off the subconscious habit of seeing the world as if it were framed. The unchecked Downs stretch away in three directions and the sea recedes into the haze where it merges with the sky.

# Unstable Boundary

If there is a frame here, it is the cliffs themselves.[13] The Seven Sisters hold in the Downs. Approaching by boat or standing at the foot of the cliffs we see only the beginning of the land. In the imagination that suggestion of green extends to encompass the whole country, Shakespeare's 'precious stone set in the silver sea'.[14]

The philosopher Jacques Derrida has paid particular attention to those features of artworks that may go unnoticed, apparently secondary to their actual subject, and all his examples have some quality reminiscent of the cliffs.[15] There are the colonnades that draw your attention to the form of a building, the marble drapery partly concealing a classical nude but at the same time emphasising her nakedness, and, most obviously, the frame around a picture. All are somehow distinct from but intrinsic to their subjects. Cliffs too are both a part of the land and separate from it.

Littoral zones are often written about as shifting and unstable, leaving no clear beginning and end to the land. Clearly this is true of the Seven Sisters, where the shelf of rock from which the cliffs rise is exposed and then covered with the tide. But it is the nature of cliffs that they maintain the illusion of a decisive boundary which the sea cannot cross. The soft hills, so expressive of traditional notions of the Beautiful, are held apart from their opposite, the Sublime and formless sea. On a calm day the landscape conveys a sense of order and balance, with the Channel and the Downs coexisting peacefully. But they remain in a state of suspense and mutual attraction, waiting only to be brought together in a storm when the waves rise up and the land is temporarily inundated.

# Delightful Turf

In 1882, his health beginning to decline with the onset of tuberculosis, the nature writer Richard Jefferies came to live in Sussex and take walks on the Downs. At Beachy Head, a little way back from the edge of the cliff, he found a perfect spot to repose. The grass, he wrote, 'washed by wind and rain, sun-dried and dew-scented, is a couch prepared with thyme to rest on.'[16]

Jefferies' contemporaries found the grass here particularly appealing. W. H. Hudson explained that 'on turning up a piece of turf the innumerable fibrous interwoven roots have the appearance of cocoa-nut matting. It is indeed this thick layer of interlaced fibres that gives the turf its springiness, and makes it so delightful to walk upon.'[17] Sir John Lubbock also found it 'delightful' and a source of national pride. Turf, he wrote, 'is peculiarly English, and no turf is more delightful than that of the Downs, delightful to ride on, to sit on, or to walk on.'[18] Lubbock himself cannot have spent too much time lying around on the grass; when not at his bank or in Parliament, he was writing on everything from the habits of ants, bees and wasps to the origins of civilisation. But we should be grateful to him, as the politician who introduced the Bank Holiday, enabling the rest of us time to enjoy the manifold pleasures of turf.

In summer this grass resembles a *mille-fleur* tapestry, dotted with purple clover, sea pink, eye-bright, centaury and wild thyme. Strangely it is the very thinness of the soil up here that we can thank for this: a deeper layer would be overrun with tall grasses. At the cliff edge you can see how much of it comprises small chalk stones, shining out from the dark earth. The name for this type of soil, rendzina, is derived from an old Polish word that describes the clinking, chattering sound made by a plough pulled through stony ground. If the Downs here seem landscaped for our comfort we can thank those Stone Age farmers who felled the woods and exposed what was then a much thicker layer of earth to the elements.

# Purifying Air

In places the turf at the edge of the cliff has been stripped bare by the ceaseless sea breeze. On the path behind the Coastguard Cottages a small hawthorn tree has been sculpted by this relentless motion of air across the Downs. It points like a flag inland, towards the north-east, in the direction of the prevailing winds.[19]

At Beachy Head, Richard Jefferies found that 'the great headland and the whole rib of the promontory is wind-swept and washed with air; the billows of the atmosphere roll over it.'[20] A century before the fashion for sea bathing began, Robert Burton was writing in his *Anatomy of Melancholy* of the benefit to mind and body of the 'sharp purifying air, which comes from the sea.'[21] Coming here I always anticipate feeling better for this washing. On a bright day the cliffs shine like porcelain or the white tiled walls of a pool. The salt wind flows across their surfaces, exfoliating any loose particles of chalk. Squalls shower rain on them which then sinks away and evaporates with the returning sun.

The notion of 'forest bathing' has become popular recently in Japan and Korea, where a short stay among the trees is recommended as a form of preventative therapy. Bathing encapsulates the idea of restorative contact with nature. You can immerse yourself in a forest, but you expose yourself on a cliff. Here the land bordering the sea has been cleansed of trees. It is a place to temporarily step away from the world, rather than find a deeper connection with it.

# Inverted Cascade

The wind is never constant. The poet Robert Bridges described it as if it were a wild beast, blindly roaming the Downs. Rearing 'upright at the cliff, to the gullies and rifts he stands; / And his conquering surges scour out over the lands.'[22] On the cliffs, the power of the wind increases the sense of risk. The closer you get to the edge, the more aware you become of it.

In Thomas Hardy's novel *A Pair of Blue Eyes*, the knowledgeable Henry Knight takes it upon himself to explain to his companion Elfride the force of the wind rushing up from the sea.

> "Over that edge," said Knight, "where nothing but vacancy appears, is a moving compact mass. The wind strikes the face of the rock, runs up it, rises like a fountain to a height far above our heads, curls over us in an arch, and disperses behind us. In fact, an inverted cascade is there—as perfect as the Niagara Falls—but rising instead of falling, and air instead of water. Now look here."
>
> Knight threw a stone over the bank, aiming it as if to go onward over the cliff. Reaching the verge, it towered into the air like a bird, turned back, and alighted on the ground behind them. They themselves were in a dead calm.[23]

Then, standing up to lean over the bank, Knight's hat is sucked off by the wind. '"That's the backward eddy, as I told you," he cried, and vanished over the little bank after his hat. Elfride waited one minute; he did not return. She waited another, and there was no sign of him.'

He was below, hanging from the cliff. Hardy's readers too were left in suspense, until the next edition of *Tinsley's Magazine*, in what has been called the first cliff hanger.

# Falling Stone

The scientific properties of a falling stone are the subject of a curious eighteenth century poem that appeared in a publication called *The Ladies' Diary: or, Woman's Almanack*. This journal carried mathematical puzzles written in verse. In one of them, readers were asked to estimate the height of a cliff from the time it took a 'pondr'ous weight' to fall. Rather than describe the landscape in geometrical terms the poem talks of cliffs whose 'furrow'd front with visage ghastly pale, / Frowns at the billows of every boist'rous gale.' Perhaps such details were meant to distract the reader. The majority of the Diary's correspondents, armed with knowledge of 'the descent of weight, and motion of sound', plumped for an answer of 670 feet.[24]

Near Hope Gap, I throw a small flint over the edge, wondering whether it will sound out distinctly. There is nothing, just the wind in my ears. No splash of water or rattle of stones. For a moment I am tempted to try again with a coin, picturing it one day being picked up again, worn and discoloured by the tide. Or perhaps it would never be found, the years slowly grinding it away. Pennies dropped into wells and fountains for good luck lie at the bottom glinting under the water. Throwing something over a cliff is a means of letting go of it completely.

In the memorable final scene of *Quadrophenia*, when its hero Jimmy, a disillusioned young mod, rides over the cliffs just east of here, the soundtrack is suspended and the moped falls slowly in complete silence before crashing onto the rocks below. This is not suicide though. At the start of the film, in a flash forward, you see Jimmy walking back inland from the cliff edge. He has jumped off before reaching the limit of the land, leaving behind him the remnants of his former life, buckled and broken at the foot of the cliff.

# Scattered Ashes

The association of cliffs and suicide, from classical myth to the deaths at Beachy Head, must arise from the way they both constitute an end point, the place at which it is impossible to travel any further. Beyond this threshold there is nothing but the flat expanse of the sea. Is there some desire to encounter death that draws us to places like this? Perhaps the beauty of it all convinces us that death itself need not be a bleak prospect.

I have thought of asking to have my own ashes scattered here. The symbolism is obvious: a return to the amniotic sea and a state of unconsciousness; the soul departing the land like a seabird borne away on the wind; a final journey over the waters to somewhere out beyond the horizon. Maybe it would seem too grandiloquent a gesture. I cannot help recalling that scene in *The Big Lebowski* where the mortal remains of The Dude's friend fail to reach the Pacific Ocean, and the look on his face as the wind's eddy catches the ashes and blows them back all over him. Better perhaps to have your ashes cast into the sea from a boat and have them sink gradually to the bottom, like the shells of the coccoliths that eventually came to constitute the chalk cliffs.

When Friedrich Engels died in 1895, his ashes were taken down to Eastbourne by Marx's daughter Eleanor and three friends. They hired a rowing boat and sailed six miles out from Beachy Head to consign his memory to the sea. There is a poignant contrast here with his old comrade, whose granite tomb at Highgate became a world famous monument.[25] There it is surrounded by rows of marble headstones. The same forces eroding the sea cliffs are gradually effacing the names of the deceased.

# Memorial Cliffs

Here on the grass slopes there are wooden benches with brief dedications. They face out to sea, slowly weathering to grey. My favourite inscription is this: 'Frank Martin 1906-1985 / Gone for a cup of tea and a / Slide down the banisters'. Others simply record names, or have a brief message: 'We Miss You', 'Thanks Pal'.

The first benches here have just one name, but demand is such that the more recent ones have several. There is a limit to the number of benches a landscape can have before it starts to resemble too closely a municipal park. On one Cornish headland I walked past a row of ten benches and the coast path at that point had the sad look of an empty station platform. I wonder how long the benches here will remain on this eroding coastline. Already those by the edge of the path are tilting downhill and it is impossible to rest comfortably on them. They give the impression of being dragged inexorably seawards as the thin surface soil is repeatedly washed by rain.

The view itself was turned into a memorial to two men, soldiers who had no particular connection with the Seven Sisters. After the First World War their surviving brother's bequest to the National Trust asked that a series of monuments be erected to their memory. Sites and buildings were to be chosen 'so far as may be possible within reasonably easy access of London'.[26] There are others in Kent, Surrey, Bedfordshire and at Sutton Place in Hackney. Situated on these pleasant grassy slopes the monument to these men is a permanent *memento mori*. It is impossible to pass it on a Seven Sisters walk without thinking, however briefly, of death. *Et in Arcadia Ego*.

# Unchecked View

Not far from this memorial, there is a monument to the preservation of this landscape. It was erected by The Society of Sussex Downsmen 'in appreciation of the generosity of William Charles Campbell Esq' whose donations preserved Crowlink Valley for the nation in 1926. This successful public appeal was prompted by fears that the Seven Sisters would become another Peacehaven (a site of such notorious ugliness that it was chosen by Graham Greene for the climactic scene in *Brighton Rock* where the gangster Pinkie, blinded by vitriol, falls over the edge of the cliff). Without the opposition of local groups and landowners we might today have had to look over the roofs and driveways of a 'Motorists Estate Deluxe' planned by the developer Carew Davies-Gilbert.

Now when I look across the Seven Sisters, from Haven Brow to Went Hill and on to the western edge of Beachy Head, the only structure I can see is the old lighthouse, Belle Tout. Over the centuries though, there have existed buildings of various kinds here, temporary or made to last, all now vanished.

One of the earliest references to this coastline is in the *Mariner's Mirrour*, a collection of sea charts compiled by Lucas Janszoon Waghenaer, first published in Holland in 1584 and translated into English four years later. It includes a small drawing of the 'Coast of Beache with the Seven Cliffes or hilles' and above these cliffs you can see two windmills and a small tower.[27] These are all long gone, as is the flagpole put up by the Preventive men to deter smugglers that gave its name to one of the Sisters, Flagstaff Point. A coastguard station was built at Crowlink, but it too has been lost as the cliffs retreated. The eye can now glide unimpeded over the Seven Sisters, with nothing to indicate that they have ever had anything built on them.

# Eye Catcher

Construction of the lighthouse Belle Tout began in 1829, partly funded by John 'Mad Jack' Fuller, MP for Sussex. Fuller's other building projects had included an obelisk, a Greek temple, a conical structure designed to resemble a church spire and the pyramid under which he would be buried. When Belle Tout eventually came into service it soon became evident that its light was too high up to be seen by vessels close to the rocks, especially when sea mists closed in. And so in 1902 the Beachy Head lighthouse was built at the bottom of the cliffs, leaving Belle Tout no more than a landmark, another of Fuller's follies. This is how it now functions at Seven Sisters, as an 'eye catcher' on the brow of the furthest visible hill.

When erosion threatened Belle Tout in 1999 it was moved physically back from the brink using hydraulic jacks. The Coastguard Cottages above Cuckmere Haven have also been shored up with a wall of grey concrete. However, you cannot see this when you walk along the cliffs; it has no more effect on the view than a repair to the back of a picture frame. As Marek Kohn points out in *Turned Out Nice*, his recent book on global warming, a rise in sea levels will increase erosion and necessitate further fortification of these buildings. Eventually 'the protected section will start to stand proud of the cliff line, and as time goes on, the cottages will look increasingly like the battlements on top of a bastion'.[28]

These cottages appear in countless photographs, increasingly integral to the aesthetics of this landscape. As Kohn says, they are 'the figures to which the Seven Sisters act as background: they feature that way in the photograph on the cover of the Ordnance Survey map, and in the film *Atonement*.' But they cannot hold out against the sea forever and one day they will be moved, or left to fall, leaving the cliff line here free of any buildings.

# Meanders

Behind the Coastguard Cottages the path leads down towards a cattle grid and a view of the River Cuckmere's curves. This is not the best vantage point to see the meanders. For that you need to look back this way from the hill at Exceat, the view Eric Ravilious painted in *Cuckmere Haven* (1939). He showed the river entering the floodplain and describing a wide 2 shape before exiting between the low slopes of the Downs. Bill Brandt took a remarkable photograph of a similar view, in which the river is an abstract path of light, with nothing to indicate it is a real place beyond a faint silvery sheen that reveals the grass in front of the camera.

I stop for a moment to look inland at the river slowly meandering over the valley. It seems reluctant to leave, until it is rushed through the artificial channel that takes it to the sea. There is a network of smaller streams too. Some of them are drainage ditches, arranged in a geometric pattern; others appear to have chosen their own course. On the river bank there is a curving white line of exposed chalk, a natural meandering form echoing that of the river. It reminds me of a brushstroke or an artist's signature.

Walking here once, my attention was caught by a movement in the grass and I saw an adder, small but unmistakable, sliding away from me. Adders are so common that an ancient Neolithic trackway just north of here is known as Snake Hill Path. All around the Seven Sisters you see tall stems of viper's bugloss with their petals opening like a snake's mouth to reveal long reddish stamens. The Cuckmere is occasionally referred to in books as The Snake River, although I have never heard anyone use that name. Seeing an adder though, it was impossible not to compare its curving motion to the serpentine river.

# Future Days

The meanders may well disappear under plans to let this valley resume a more natural state. We would then have to remember this river as it was through the images of artists like Ravilious and Brandt. I picture them hanging in museums next to photographs made by land artists to record their temporary sculptures, those spirals and circles made in the certain knowledge they will gradually lose their forms.

In Marek Kohn's book he imagines a future for Cuckmere Valley in which climate change has been accompanied by public acceptance that the meanders captured by Ravilious and Brandt cannot be preserved forever. A different kind of aesthetic appreciation may develop as 'a chromatic shift from rain-green to sea-green' takes place, with plants adapted to saltwater replacing the grass that covers the floodplain now. Above the river, there could be new colours too: 'birds with tones of sunrise in their plumage, somehow simultaneously a misty orange and a deep nimbus violet. These are purple herons, brought to the south coast by the growing warmth.'[29]

The Cuckmere Valley is hard to return to without feelings of what has been called 'solastalgia', the distress and sense of loss caused by environmental damage. Solastalgia is felt most intensely when rapid change ruptures the connections we feel with a familiar landscape. Things may seem superficially stable here, but you sense something coming. The flood plain, cliffs and beach are all in a state of suspense. An unseasonable feeling of warmth in the air can lead thoughts quickly to rising sea levels and damaged ecosystems. Richard Jefferies and W. H. Hudson both wrote novels set in the future, but their essays on the Downs could not foresee the way they are experienced today with an underlying note of sadness.

# Mutable Beach

Looking down now at the beach I realise that it has visibly altered in the last year. The Cuckmere's final path to the sea has been diverted to the west, flowing parallel to the beach and creating a pebble spit. At first I assume that this is part of some conservation plan, but then I see the battered wooden breakwaters and realise that the sea has done this. Wooden piles have been swept away and there are gaps where horizontal planks used to keep the pebbles in place. Now the river simply flows straight through them, turning them into precarious bridges.

Of course the Cuckmere has continuously changed its course. In the 1587 Armada Survey it entered the sea just under the Seven Sisters but a map of 1757 shows it having migrated all the way to the other side of the valley. It is a shock nevertheless to see such a change in the space of twelve months.

The mutability of this coast was noted in a book published in 1927 that set out to describe the county in 'various moods and seasons', *Everyman's Sussex*. 'On stormy days such as this no one can tell what the aspect of the Haven will be when the breakers draw off their forces.'[30] A hundred years earlier Charles Lyell referred to Sussex storm beaches in his great work, the *Principles of Geology*. Reflecting on the way the sea had cut away the site of a supposedly Roman earthwork, he imagined geologists in future centuries reconstructing the way the landscape used to look from historical records.[31] If storms become more frequent the configuration of this beach will look different each time we come to visit it.

# Vibrant Matter

There is an essay, one of several written by the anthropologist Tim Ingold to critique static, pictorial notions of landscape, in which he describes a field trip to a beach.[32] All was in flux that day: the surging breakers, the wheeling seabirds and the rain that drenched Ingold's students as he asked them to contemplate their 'weather-world'.

Focus your attention on the churning sea and it is relatively easy to recall that the environment is a complex set of fluid processes. But what happens if you turn back to look at the solid white cliffs? It is possible to consider them in the same way: 'sea-ing' the land, as Ingold puts it. Do this and the Seven Sisters no longer seem to stand apart from their world. Instead you start to experience land and sea as part of the same sphere of forces, constantly moving with the weather and the seasons.

The clouds drift, the pebbles shift beneath your feet. These stones are part of the weather-world and are subject to change on a larger scale too. 'A zone of transformative processes set in train through the interplay of wind, water and stone, within a field of cosmic forces such as those responsible for the tides.' This is how Ingold refers to the beach.

It is only at the level of human perception that the cliffs are stationary. The chalk is vibrant matter. Everything here is in motion.

# Rockfalls

Resting beneath the cliffs, I start to recognise signs of their instability. The photographer Jem Southam has described this experience, which for him was a moment of creative epiphany.

> My attention was gradually pulled from the spectacle and roar of the waves to the trickle of sounds coming from the cliff face behind me. Remaining still and watching intently, I became aware of the tiny rivulets of particles that were sliding their way down the cliff onto the beach below. Every so often a larger rock would slip away, tumble down and thud into the sand. The longer I stood the more I became aware that these processes were almost as frequent, though not as rhythmic, as the waves pounding the shore. Into the imaginative space opened up by this experience came, firstly, the idea of the surface of the earth as a permanently fluid space (where the driving forces of erosion – gravity, rain, wind and wave – shape the land through time), and secondly, how a still photographic image might provide a unique medium through which to examine and reflect on such matters.[33]

The result was a series of photographs he called *Rockfalls*. Among them is a cascade of chalk that came down at Birling Gap, just beyond the Seven Sisters.

Small but persistent processes of erosion are happening all over the landscape. Sometimes it is the activity of animals, like the rabbits whose burrows undermined a World War Two pillbox to the extent that it had to be restored in the 1990s. Sometimes it is the weather, with frostbitten flints falling from the cliffs like nuts from trees.[34] The cliffs themselves represent ruin on a grand scale. Here the hills have been reduced to nothing but pebbles and scattered rocks by the repeated abrasions of storms and breakers, and by slow, imperceptible weathering.

# Changing Cliffscape

The cliffs, I have read, recede on average about 30-40cm each year, although estimates vary.[35] How different would they have looked to Jefferies and Hudson, or to the smugglers and revenue men of the eighteenth century, or the sailors who passed them for centuries before they came to be called the Seven Sisters?

The late sixteenth century drawing of 'the Seven Cliffes' on *The Mariner's Mirrour* map looks very different to the modern shoreline. This may be less a case of inaccurate cartography than it is a reflection of the changes the coast has undergone. As the sea has been patiently chiselling away at the cliffs it has simplified their forms, discarding a sequence of chalk pinnacles. Old texts sometimes refer to 'The Charleses' and it seems that these were not the cliffs themselves, but towers of chalk that had been washed away by the end of the nineteenth century. The term Charleses sounds as if should date from Stuart times, although the word ending could be an example of the double 's' that was a distinctive feature of the old Sussex dialect. The chalk towers may originally have been known as 'The Seven Men' (Churls).

There were seven oaks once that gave their name to the village of Sevenoaks in Kent and they have been blown down and replaced many times.[36] How exposed to serious storm damage are the Seven Sisters themselves? The gradually weakening chalk stacks that once stood in front of the cliffs became as vulnerable as old trees. Storms will continue to move the Cuckmere River and dislodge boulders of chalk but the Seven Sisters themselves will remain for longer, receding only gradually, until the sea reaches so far inland that their identities merge.

# Formless Stones

At Hope Gap, I saw a group of rough chalk boulders lying dumped on the beach, seemingly unwanted by land or sea. Here, at Cuckmere Haven, the expanse of pebbles is grey, like the gravel people use to turn front gardens into driveways for their second cars. Some of the rock is covered in a pelt of vivid green seaweed. Everywhere the exposed chalk is pockmarked and stained. Bordering the sea is a stretch of tangled black kelp. None of these things lift the heart. Rock pools always hold out a certain promise but I have been here on overcast days when the sun refuses to dance on their surface and they are merely sumps of cold salt water abandoned by the tide.

Before the fashion for sea bathing and a taste for rugged scenery developed in the eighteenth century, beaches like this provoked active feelings of disgust. As Alain Corbin points out in his classic study of this transformation in taste, *The Lure of the Sea*, there were no beaches in the Garden of Eden.[37] The pastoral ideal, celebrated in poetry and art, was a scene of soft grass, shady trees, fragrant flowers, abundant fruit and clear spring water. What nymphs would choose to sit on windswept slimy rocks and listen to the shrieking gulls? The beach was a place where things were washed up. Human detritus, fish and animal carcasses, the melancholy remnants of wrecked ships.

Cliffs allow us to experience the beach at a distance. Detritus lying abject and exposed on the foreshore is indiscernible. From the Seven Sisters you look down not on stones but at harmonious bands of colour - grey, yellow, green, black - that blur together at their edges. I suspect that walkers on the coast path barely see the beach at all. At high tide it is no more than an outline. At low tide it is negative space between the green hills, framed by their white cliffs, and the blue water, fringed with white foam.

# Distant Ships

Before you approach them the old wooden piles of the breakwaters seem to be natural outgrowths of the beach, rising from the shallows like the remains of a petrified forest. But they are matted with polypropylene rope in orange, yellow and cyan that tie this landscape to the world of industrial fishing and container transportation. You could try to disentangle them but more would arrive with the next storm tide.

Today the sea is calm and quiet, pale grey-blue with a sheen where the sun is directly above it. There are hardly any boats, although I can see the Newhaven ferry in the distance, slowly getting smaller. It sails much less frequently these days of course, but has been making the journey to France since 1847 and has the minor distinction of being the first roll-on, roll-off cross-Channel car ferry. Now there are rumours that the French will stop subsidising it and the service will close.

Beyond the ferry, the silhouette of a container ship seems barely to be moving. Impossible to know what it is carrying as it makes its way, linking who knows what parts of the global supply chain. It is a descendent of a merchant ship that the poet Charlotte Smith could see from Beachy Head two hundred years ago, out beyond the more familiar local fishing boats,

> ... more remote, and like a dubious spot
> Just hanging in the horizon, laden deep,
> The ship of commerce richly freighted, makes
> Her slower progress, on her distant voyage.[38]

# Nympha

In ancient Greece the summer sailing season began and ended when the Pleiades were in conjunction with the sun. Between these dates the seas were easily navigable. The seven nymphs, transformed into stars, were thus associated with the safety of ships. At certain times of the year they were a warning to keep away from the sea.

These Seven Sisters have witnessed many ships in trouble. One was called the *Nympha Americana*: pursued by bad weather she lost her way and perished before the Seven Sisters in 1747. Thirty crewmen died that day when the foc'stle overturned. In an old engraving, *A View of the Wreck of the Nympha, A Spanish Prize*, the beach under the cliffs can be seen full of people salvaging whatever they could find. This Hogarthian drama of greed and folly is hard to reconcile with a vision of this place as a scene of tranquil beauty. The *Sussex Advertiser and Lewes Journal* described what happened:

> Never was known such a multitude of people at a wreck before, many of whom by drinking too plentifully of a cask of very strong brandy, which they found upon the beach, were intoxicated and afterwards *perished* by death, while numbers of others loaded themselves and some of their horses with the goods that were thrown up by the tide from the said wreck tho' there is a party of soldiers sent to prevent so abominable a practice, and notwithstanding they have shot one man dead, yet people will continue to venture.[39]

# Traces

Few traces of this coast's shipwrecks remain, but on certain days in spring at low tides it is still possible to see the remains of the *Coonatto*. This clipper, bound for London with a cargo of copper ingot and wool, had sailed all the way from Australia only to be driven onshore here in 1876. Fragments of its wood now stick out of the beach at low angles.

There are other remnants. Rusting iron fragments projecting from the sea beyond the mouth of the Cuckmere belonged to a German sail ship, the *Polynesia*. And to the west of Birling Gap the remains of two vessels that saw action in the First World War lie side by side: a steam propelled freighter, the *Ushla*, and the captured German U-boat 121. If war cast these cliffs as a national defence, the wrecks remind us that they will not favour one side over another.

The Seven Sisters may never witness another big wreck now that navigating the sea roads has been de-risked with technology designed to plot a safe course through changeable weather systems. But these efficiently programmed journeys could still be disrupted, hacked into or wilfully diverted off course. New imperatives too may lead people out onto this sea, attempting the crossing from France in fragile, overfull boats.

I can see a fragment of worn wood half buried in the rubble of rocks. It is probably nothing really, just some tide-softened piece of litter, but could have floated here as flotsam long years ago. There is no way of knowing, its origins having been utterly effaced by the sea.

# Layers of Time

When Richard Jefferies looked down on the view from Beachy Head he felt the reality of late Victorian England slipping away from him. 'The sea knows no time and no era; you cannot tell what century it is from the face of the sea. A Roman trireme suddenly rounding the white edge-line of chalk, borne on wind and oar from the Isle of Wight towards the gray castle at Pevensey (already old in olden days), would not seem strange.'[40]

Rudyard Kipling also imagined a landscape little changed in two millennia. His cliffscape in the poem 'Sussex' has come to represent the national character.

> Clean of officious fence or hedge,
> Half-wild and wholly tame,
> The wise turf cloaks the white cliff-edge
> As when the Romans came.[41]

Turning their backs on expanding cities and land given over to manufacturing it was easy for these writers to come here and imagine an unbroken thread of history. Now we know that industrialisation has brought change to the world so profound it can be measured on the scale of geological time. The cliffs' pristine chalk strata call attention to the way our own layer of time has been polluted. Frozen air preserved in ice cores contains mercury, calcium, black carbon and radioactive elements. It is still possible to look out to sea and imagine a trireme pulling past the Seven Sisters but harder now to draw solace from a feeling of continuity with the land as it was when the Romans came.

# Smuggler's Bottom

Kipling's novel *Puck of Pook's Hill*, like his poem 'Sussex', moves in and out of history, as figures from the past are summoned by the elf Puck to tell their tales. This desire to celebrate 'our island story' can be viewed as typical of its time, but the idea that the past can surface through the landscape continues to resonate, fitting our contemporary enthusiasm for buried histories and hauntings. [42]

There is a local legend that links Puck with the nearby cliff at Seaford Head, where a hard-to-reach ledge called Puck Church Parlour can be seen at the end of a cleft. [43] Puck, the mischievous nature sprite, is always an ambiguous figure. There are stories of him leading travellers astray in woods with fairy lights, like fires lit on clifftops to lure unsuspecting ships onto the rocks.

Puck appears again in Kipling's sequel, *Rewards and Fairies*. In one of its stories the children walk down to a gap in the chalk cliffs where they meet a Sussex smuggler called Pharaoh Lee. Stories of smuggling are common to all coastal landscapes and have become part of the mythology of Sussex. There is a Puckish quality to figures like James Pettit, alias Jevington Jigg, whose gang used landing beaches at Birling Gap and Crowlink (a place still called Smuggler's Bottom). [44]

In the eighteenth century you could drink a glass of Hollands gin advertised as 'Genuine Crow Link' that had made its way to London via hiding holes in a farmhouse behind the Seven Sisters. The cliffs could be scaled with ladders and ropes, and the contraband winched up using horses. On one occasion a smuggler was forced to run from the scene when a patrol appeared, leaving a dozen tubs to crash down onto the beach, soaking it in forty gallons of spirit. Thus history percolates into the stones. Most of it is washed away but some of the stories adhere.

# The Great Flood

I have only been on the beach a few minutes when I see a pebble with an intriguing circular pattern - a fossil echinoid. Such traces of the prehistory of this coast are easy to find: small objects that open up vast stretches of time. Human history is like the shallow layer of soil on the edge of the cliffs, with aeons of white chalk beneath. Scratch the cliff face and you release all that is left of those years as a fine dust that quickly disappears in the air.

Charlotte Smith's long poem 'Beachy Head', published posthumously in 1807, begins in the distant past. Rather than contemplate the slow accumulation of time, she pictures the day when a great flood rushed 'between / The rifted shores, and from the continent / Eternally divided this green isle.'[45] Reclining on the summit of the cliffs, the poet lets her 'Fancy go forth' to encounter the Sublime in two of its aspects. The fearful dynamical power of nature, expressed in the sudden deluge, is as overwhelming to the mind as the immeasurable stretches of time that separate us from it.

This barely conceivable event is something contemporary scientists think they have detected in the deep scars revealed by sonar on the Channel bed. At that time a narrow isthmus called the Weald-Artois ridge, possibly thirty metres higher than the current sea level, linked Britain to the continent. The exact cause of this inundation is unclear.[46] In Smith's poem it is 'the Omnipotent' who 'stretch'd forth his arm, and rent the solid hills.' Modern palaeo-researchers think an earthquake may have breached the isthmus, causing water from a huge lake to the north, fed by earlier forms of the Rhine and Thames, to suddenly discharge its water in a flood that may have lasted months.

# Sheep on the Summit

From the beach I climb the steep path up Haven Brow, first of the Seven Sisters, and at its summit I am able again to see land and sea in every direction. There are a few sheep up here, still white forms in the distance, seemingly as ancient as the chalk. It is easy to forget that they are kept within a farm, by a fence that the eye barely registers, limited in where they can graze and prevented from straying too close to the edge.

They were not always so carefully protected. Charlotte Smith noted that 'sometimes in thick weather the sheep feeding on the summit of the cliff, miss their footing and are killed by the fall.'[47] There is a famous Pre-Raphaelite painting by William Holman Hunt, showing a flock perilously close to falling.[48] The title it was given, *Strayed Sheep*, may have been influenced by John Ruskin's *Notes on the Construction of Sheepfolds* (1851), where Christians are portrayed as strayed sheep. Ruskin expressed dismay at the persistence of Catholicism in Europe, with 'Christ's truth' only apparent among 'the white cliffs of England and white crests of the Alps'.[49]

The Seven Sisters have the austere lines and plain white surfaces of a Protestant church interior. They stand above the world, leading our vision up and beyond it. But their whiteness represents an unattainable purity. Ruskin would have found no guidance here. His remedy for disunity among the different strands of Protestantism was that they should go back and read the Scriptures.

Different breeds of sheep lived together here at the Seven Sisters Sheep Centre. However, this privately-owned collection has recently closed.[50] The sheep near where I am standing on Haven Brow all resemble each other. They graze quietly, standing alone or clustered in small groups. It would be possible to walk here looking out to sea and hardly notice them at all.

# Withdrawing Roar

Victorian religious uncertainties infuse another celebrated painting of chalk cliffs by Hunt's contemporary William Dyce. *Pegwell Bay, Kent – a Recollection of October 5th 1858* depicts the rock strata in loving detail. Dyce was a keen geologist and his wife and her two sisters are visible in the foreground collecting shells and fossils. This was the coast where St Augustine is said to have landed on his mission to bring Christianity to the Anglo-Saxons, but it was also now the source for new scientific thinking. In the sky above the cliffs, Dyce painted a streak of light resembling the Star of Bethlehem. It was actually Donati's Comet, visible on that date, but not to be seen from Earth again for another two thousand years.

Eight years earlier, at Dover Beach, where 'the cliffs of England stand, / Glimmering and vast', Matthew Arnold had listened to the tide retreat. It seemed to him that the Sea of Faith that once had girdled the country's shore was now beginning to go out, with 'a melancholy, long, withdrawing roar.'[51]

The nineteenth century's new understanding of the world was informed in part by the long-dead creatures preserved in cliffs like these. The rocks though are not as lifeless as they seem. Touch the Seven Sisters and you may be in contact with organisms that could withstand the vacuum of space. A fragment of the cliffs at Beer in Dorset was taken on the International Space Station and left outside for 553 days to study the effect on microbes living in it.[52] Some of them actually survived out in the glimmering vastness of space. This seems to me a source of wonder rather than melancholy. Maybe there are micro-organisms living on Donati's comet, and cliffs resembling these standing now on the edge of seas on other worlds.

# Gold on the Grass

On the brightest days, light leaps from the cliffs and their faceted surfaces draw you like unpolished diamonds. Today they are a neutral grey and the plain pebbles beneath them have an almost Zen simplicity. This feels like a place to renounce worldly goods. Here one should stand empty-handed before the ocean, like the figure in Caspar David Friedrich's famous painting *The Monk by the Sea*. The monk appears to be standing on dunes sprinkled with grass, but there is another possible reading of the picture in which he is standing *above* the sea, on one of the chalk headlands of Rügen, a shoreline that resembles the Seven Sisters.

'Walking on the Cliff' is an allegorical poem written by Andrew Young in the late nineteen-thirties, when he was minister of the Presbyterian Church at Hove. In it he observes a blackcap, 'Perched like a miser on the yellow furze / High over Birling Gap.' Intent on this bird, who sings 'Gold is a blessing not a curse', the poet almost finds himself inadvertently stepping over the cliff edge.[53]

This is not a place to seek real gold, although in 1806 a Bronze Age hoard was discovered in the cliff face of Beachy Head by a one-eyed fisherman named Jumper Hutches.[54] You can still be struck though by the gold of the furze, scattered over the turf and marking the edges of the sheep fields. There is a story, probably apocryphal, that the great Swedish botanist Linnaeus fell to his knees and offered thanks when he first viewed a field of flowering furze in England. It is mentioned in Arthur Beckett's *The Spirit of the Downs*, which has a chapter devoted to the simple beauty of furze. 'Here is gold on the grass greater than the treasure of Giaconda. Why toil and delve and sweat for riches when they are here – laid bare on the turf?'[55]

# A Lone Hermit

At one time a chapel stood on the Seven Sisters, with its light shining forth as a warning to sailors. At Seaford Head, there was a small hermitage used by a recluse called Peter who received royal protection in 1272, possibly for providing a lookout service.[56] The lonely vigil held by a lighthouse keeper has much in common with the eremitic life that drew early Christians to isolated cliffs and islands. Combining both roles may have helped resolve a persistent doubt that leaving behind the world represented a retreat from humanity, an abandonment of their responsibilities to others.

A mild version of this dilemma can make a solitary walker feel uneasy. But getting away from things for just a day, finding space to think, is not a rejection of other people. Giving attention to the landscape, becoming attuned to its particularities, noticing its variety, feeling the weather and sensing the way the land changes as you walk over it; all this heightens the capacity for responding generously towards the world, including that part of it temporarily left behind. And, in any case, you will not go far on the Seven Sisters without encountering other walkers.

In the early eighteenth century, before Belle Tout was constructed, there was a parson who achieved some local renown by spending nights in a cave at Beachy Head, sheltering from the wind whilst he watched to see if any sailors needed assistance.[57] Writing thirty years after first hearing stories about this 'lone Hermit', Charlotte Smith imagined him wandering on the beach where

> He learn'd to auger from the clouds of heaven,
> And from the changing colours of the sea,
> And sullen murmurs of the hollow cliffs.[58]

Thus over the years he had come to be able to read nature so well that he could predict its moods, and through this knowledge he could come to the aid of other people.

# Prospect and refuge

For sailors caught in storms, these hills were more than just dry land. Their folds respond to an innate desire for a safe haven, while their heights offer a place from which we can see widely in all directions. Geographers have speculated that pleasure in a landscape comes from an atavistic attraction to places where it is possible to see without being seen: prospect-refuge theory.[59]

During the Second World War, a morale-boosting poster was produced with the message *'your BRITAIN – fight for it now'*. It shows a shepherd following a line of sheep in the direction of an old farmstead safely nestled among the trees. Beyond him, the Downs offer wide open spaces and a glimpse of blue sea. On the summit of the hill is a small tower, a secondary symbol that itself offers both prospect and refuge. It is recognisable as the old lighthouse overlooking Beachy Head, Belle Tout.

Looking east from this point, the cliffs represent an extended sequence of prospects and the sea beyond is wide open to the horizon. It has to be said though that around me there is only low vegetation - little by way of cover – which perhaps reinforces the strong temptation to find a spot to recline on the grass.

The surrounding hills may be exposed and largely treeless, but there is something comforting and protective about the shape of the Downs here. Francis William Bourdillon, a poet who lived in Eastbourne in the late nineteenth century, found their slopes 'softly rounded as a mother's arm about a cradle.'[60] They offer shelter from the sea, with its storms and dangers.

I sit back and look out from the highest of the Seven Sisters, which stands protectively over the mouth of the river. Refuge and prospect are combined in the name it has been given, Haven Brow.

# Dragon's teeth

A striking photograph exists from the Second World War of soldiers running through the surf, towards this beach, beneath the Seven Sisters. Behind them is the seemingly impregnable rock stretching into the distance. They look as if they were part of an invading army. In fact this was a company of the Canadian infantrymen stationed here during the war, taking part in an assault training exercise.[61]

Cuckmere Haven was an opening in the defensive line of cliffs. It had been identified by the Germans as a landing site for their Operation Sea Lion. To counter the threat, the valley floor was transformed with barbed wire, land mines, anti-tank ditches and gun emplacements. The small concrete pyramids that can still be seen here were designed to impede German tanks as they headed up the estuary. These are known as 'dragon's teeth' and I imagine them sown across the landscape like those in the story of Jason and the Argonauts, ready to spring into life to defend the Golden Fleece.

By September 1940 Hitler had concluded that an invasion of Britain was not feasible and in the end these defences never had to be used. They had to be maintained though, for who knew how the war would turn? That same month four men lost their lives laying mines on the beach.

'*Your BRITAIN – fight for it now*' – would it have meant much to the Canadian soldiers stationed here? Perhaps those young men accustomed to the forests and lakes of a different continent did feel stirred by something special in this landscape. What they were protecting may have been hard to define, but it was present in the vulnerable hills behind them. As they studied the sea from their pillboxes near the river mouth, they could take strength from the towering cliffs lined up on either side.

# Cleft castle

In June 1940 the war artist Paul Nash painted a watercolour which he called *Under the Cliff*. A Heinkel bomber lies broken on the beach beneath a grey sky. From a low angle the tail of the plane looks as high as the cliffs, but thin and fragile. In another of his paintings of downed aircraft, *The Raider on the Shore*, a German bomber can be seen lying like a dead bird between the breakwaters. The cliffs are a sequence of eroded profiles retreating to the horizon and the aircraft looks as if it is gradually being washed into the sea.

The Seven Sisters are thicker than any fortress walls. They rise vertically from the solid bedrock and every few feet there are natural buttresses supporting them. One of the local poems collected by Arthur Bell in *The Book of Sussex Verse*, published on the eve of the First World War, compares their 'massy grandeur' to 'some cleft castle, which with calm disdain / still braves the outrage of inclement skies.'[62] They could, it seems, defeat anything thrown against them.

There is a drawing by the poet and artist Ian Hamilton Finlay with a descriptive title: *At the field's edge, on the vertiginous cliff-top, stood a solitary hut*. It could be a Romantic landscape, something like the distant view of Belle Tout lighthouse. But the vertiginous cliff-like form is actually an aircraft carrier and the hut is its control tower. This visual metaphor makes me wonder if a navy pilot looking down from the deck rail would experience the sense of awe I feel on a cliff edge. Probably they would picture nothing but the flight ahead of them and only after landing again, emerging from the cockpit and feeling the wind off the waves, two hundred feet below, would a sense of their own vulnerability return.

# White citadel

Haven Brow dominates the view when you stand on the beach at Cuckmere Haven. It takes longer than you would think to reach it as your pace is slowed by the grey drifts of stones. Approaching this huge weight of rock a natural sense of physical insignificance is heightened by the intimidating blankness of its dead white surface.

Centres of power are usually concealed behind such high white walls. Surely many of them have been consciously or unconsciously designed to resemble cliff-like structures. In their different ways, buildings like St. Peter's Basilica, the White House and the Bank of England are all descendants of the Acropolis, a citadel built on a cliff. 'Acron' means 'edge' and so the Acropolis was the city on the edge.

In London I often walk past the blank walls of the Ministry of Defence, which tower silently above you, their small grey windows arranged in lines like flint strata. Seagulls scavenge in their shadows and pigeons alight on the building's green roofs - rock doves that found a new home in the city.

An arbitrary power resides in cliffs. We know that rock will fall, but we do not know when. We still stand under them though, reasoning that the chances of injury are slight. Immanuel Kant saw overhanging and threatening rocks as an example of sublimity, all the more attractive for being fearful.[63] A cliff challenges us but, through reason, Kant thought, we can establish our 'pre-eminence over nature even in its immeasurability'. We see things differently now, suspicious of aesthetic pleasure that may arise from a subconscious desire to subjugate nature. Reason, we hope, will devise ways to limit our own power over the increasingly vulnerable landscape.

# Infinity Cove

I have said that white buildings can denote power, but they also have more uplifting associations. When I think of sleek white modern designs I picture them against an azure sea or a cloudless sky: catamarans and cruise liners, Concorde and Cape Canaveral. In Sussex, white is the colour of the Art Deco terminal building at Shoreham airport, opened in 1936, and the low white curve of Saltdean Lido, built further along the coast in 1937-38. Entering these we leave behind the heavy confusion of daily life and experience clean, light spaces that connect us to the elements of air and water. The cliffs have this quality too.

Sometimes when I am in the city an unexpected glimpse of clouds drifting behind a sunlit wall can recall the sensation of looking up at the cliffs. The eye is led into the sky and for a fleeting moment the white concrete side of an office block or a municipal library building provides the feeling of transcendence experienced before the Seven Sisters, bright with the light of the sea.

In recent years I have been visiting another modernist building in Sussex, the De La Warr Pavilion, which lies like a low cliff above the beach at Bexhill. Its interior walls are painted white, in keeping with its latest role as an art gallery. Such rooms are like the white backgrounds photographers use to make their subjects stand out, which have the poetic name 'infinity coves'. It is a paradoxical term, suggesting enclosure in endless space, or an inlet where the cliffs reflect each other like mirrors. At its simplest, the infinity cove is a white wall and floor, with no visible join. There is a similar effect here at the Seven Sisters when high tide reaches the foot of the cliffs and the sea reflects their surfaces, so that a swimmer beneath them is bathed in white light.

# Fata Morgana

The word Albion may derive from the word for white, in which case it could have been given to the country by sailors, sighting these cliffs from the sea.[64] Bill Brandt described in a letter the magical appearance of the Seven Sisters from the cross-Channel ferry. 'About an hour before Newhaven the Seven Sisters appear like a Fata Morgana on the horizon, brilliantly white in the afternoon sun – the sun always shines. England then looks like a small fairy island. It is an unforgettable experience and again and again a surprise for me.'[65]

When the conditions are right for a Fata Morgana, the brilliant sea glitter at the horizon is projected into the sky to create cliffs of pure light. They resemble walls of ice, frozen at the limits of vision. Nineteenth century arctic explorers were misled into thinking they were distant landmasses. Sailing towards them, they found the cliffs never got any closer but remained always ahead of them, out of reach.

'The Imaginary Iceberg' is the subject of an early poem by Elizabeth Bishop. She pictures it as a 'cloudy rock' on a sea of moving marble.[66] A year later, in 1936, the poet and clergyman Andrew Young used a similar metaphor in a poem about these Sussex cliffs. They were so white they seemed like 'frozen air'.[67] He looked up at them from the beach, where there was little to shade him from their 'blazing height'. Like the Fata Morgana they can seem to be both ice and light. If Bill Brandt saw these cliffs in the distance as the walls of a fairy island, Andrew Young, standing up close, felt himself blinded by them, like 'a soul strayed in paradise.'

# Marine Snow

The chalk near the top of the cliffs appears miraculously white: a perfect absence of colour that you rarely see in nature, except when the land is covered in fresh snow. Other limestones contain impurities and organic matter but the chalk was formed as a pure white mud in warm seas, gradually solidifying over time into cold rock.

In their slow retreat, the Seven Sisters resemble the ice sheet that covered northern Britain. I sometimes wonder what it would be like if we could experience chalk exposed over large stretches of land, like an Arctic landscape. Sandstone cliffs seem to convey a memory of desert heat, whilst chalk feels almost devoid of any warmth. Perhaps this is because it consists of skeletons, the remnants of numberless marine algae, which fell through the sea, in the words of Jacquetta Hawkes, like flakes of 'marine snow'.[68]

In her book on the geology of Britain, *A Land* (1951), Hawkes expressed the weight of time made visible in this chalk by explaining that the height of a small child standing against a cliff would span the accumulation of one hundred and twenty thousand years. The chalk, she wrote, is often 'so pure that hardly any refinement is necessary to make those white fingers which teachers use for their blackboard demonstrations, and which turn into the clouds of white dust so characteristic of the lower forms of scholastic life. If my imagination were reasonable, it would see these clouds rather than snowstorms blowing down through the Cretaceous oceans.'[69]

Scholastic life has evolved and the blackboards are gone. My own generation's teachers were the last to add a stratum of chalk dust. In all those years, so many lessons, so many words, written and erased, like forgetful snow. If the chalk is an expression of time it also represents a kind of oblivion.

# Writing in Chalk

Chalk can bring to mind both the act of writing and the whiteness of the page. Its blank, unworked state is also suggestive of the raw materials that art colours and transforms, from silk and porcelain to the plastic forms created by 3D printers. Chalk itself is a component of the gesso primer used by artists to prepare surfaces for paint. At the base of the cliffs where the rock surface is frequently wet by waves, it has been smoothed and moulded like plaster. Above, its carved white surface resembles the walls of a marble quarry.

When the artist Eric Ravilious was looking for subject matter near here, he became fascinated with a cement works that had been carved out of the Downs, creating man-made cliffs of chalk. He found everything there covered by a fine white powder.[70] His watercolours, which make use of exposed areas of paper, can seem as if they are stippled with chalk.

Small chalk stones lie scattered over the Seven Sisters. Visitors are continually arranging and rearranging them into letters that spell out messages. I have sometimes thought of this as a form of graffiti, with none of the ingenious beauty of an Andy Goldsworthy sculpture or purity of form Richard Long achieves in his stone circles. But these temporary assemblages do not last long and most are not visible at any great distance. It is hard to begrudge lovers who assemble the stones into hearts enclosing their initials. Often the messages point to distant places – SWITZERLAND, IOWA, BRASIL – as if being at the edge of England prompts travellers to remember where they have journeyed from. Sometimes just a name is left, as if the visitor wanted to sign the landscape like an artist before recording it in a photograph.

# Flint Notation

Looking along the cliffs you see lines of embedded flints separated by cracks and fissures. They resemble an indecipherable text. The notion that something could be read in the cliffs must have occurred to John Piper, whose early collage, *Beach with Starfish*, depicts the Seven Sisters using pages from the New Statesman. [71] These fragments of journalism from 1933 deal with issues that echo in the news today, even if the details have changed. Perhaps there is a metaphor in this; events come and go but the landscape of politics, like the line of the cliffs, alters more slowly, despite the occasional shocks that feel like dramatic rock falls.

In another collage, *Harbour Scene, Newhaven*, Piper represents the sea cliffs using some discarded sheet music that had been used to clean the printing presses in his studio. The patterns of flints on the Seven Sisters look like neumes, the squarish notation used in early music manuscripts. In places they trace a simple monotone, on other strata of the cliff face they become more complex or confused.

Piper was influenced by the *papier collé* of Picasso and Braque, whose compositions included newspapers and scores along with the silhouettes of guitars and bottles. But he was also inspired by the collage of materials that you see here, washed up along the beach. Collage emphasises process and those put together by Piper reminds us that the shapes and textures of the visible landscape are not fixed in place forever. We alter the beach in a small way ourselves when we pick up pebbles that catch our eye and drop them to create a new arrangement which will last only until the next wave.

# Blank Canvas

In France, the white cliffs at Étretat were a blank canvas for the succession of artists who came to paint them in the nineteenth century: Delacroix, Courbet, Monet. Monet owned a Delacroix watercolour of the landscape and arrived there himself in 1883. Guy de Maupassant, who saw him there two years later, described Monet's pursuit of the transient effects of light to readers of Paris periodical *Gil Blas*.

> Face to face with his subject, the painter lay in wait for the sun and shadows, capturing in a few brushstrokes the ray that fell or the cloud that passed. I have seen him seize a glittering shadow of light on the white cliff and fix it in a flood of yellow tone which strangely rendered the surprising and fugitive effect of that elusive and dazzling brilliance.[72]

Cliffs offer an ideal subject for the artist interested in exploring shades of grey, but Monet painted Étretat, where the rocks are as white as the Seven Sisters, in a whole spectrum of colours. One day they were dove grey against a misty sky; on another, a dark green obscured by sheets of rain. He rendered them in shades of blue barely distinguishable from the waves, in deep indigo with a low red sun behind them and in purple, set off by an extraordinary yellow and pale green sunset. In one painting, the famous chalk arch is tinged with pink and floats in a blue-green sea like a water lily.

Come here often enough, such paintings suggest, and you would see the light from sea and sky paint the Seven Sisters in all these colours. There are subtle effects, when the Downs lend their colour to the shadows on the cliff face, and spectacular ones, when the setting sun gilds the whole length of the coastline.

# The Body and the Beach

Bill Brandt visited Étretat and conceived there the idea of photographing a nude on the beach, under the cliffs. The initial results were not good enough to publish and the experience was a very cold and uncomfortable one for his partner Marjorie.[73] But the concept was one he continued to pursue in a whole series of nude studies, both in France and near the Seven Sisters at Seaford.

In these photographs, models are shown curled up like chalk boulders or stretched out, the curves of their bodies repeated in the cliffs. They are, as always with Brandt, carefully composed, even though he saw them as chance pictures, unexpected combinations of shapes and landscapes. In some of them skin looks unnaturally white, pure and idealised like marble statues, in others the flesh is given a warmer grey tone and the cold white cliff behind emphasises the softness of the models' bodies.

The nude in art is a body framed as an aesthetic object and Bill Brandt's models go to some lengths to frame themselves, concealing their individuality. Their faces are turned away, hidden by an arm or obscured by long hair pulled forward and blowing in the wind. Brandt isolates parts of the body, creating sculptural or geomorphic forms out of arms, breasts, toes and fingers, or a single ear. In one composition the model's buttock resembles a sea-smoothed rock, whilst its curve is echoed by the Seven Sisters behind. Here it is not the Downs that suggests human contours but the models who take on aspects of the landscape.

This dismemberment and objectification of women, posed painfully on the rocks and pebbles, is troubling. Rather than resting naturally, they are frozen in a state of unnatural beauty. Attempts to preserve the cliff line and retain the beautiful curve of the Cuckmere's meanders may stem from similar impulses, an urge to fetishize the landscape itself.

# Muscular Hills

There is a long tradition of artists hiding recognisable elements of the human body in clouds, mountains and rock formations. In one of Edgar Degas' drawings, for example, the form of a sleeping woman can be discerned in rounded hillocks of turf at the edge of the sea.[74] Was the land shaping itself round a particular memory? Or did its curves and mounds work on his imagination? There are subconscious reasons for responding to the particular configuration of a landscape.[75] Our deepest memories were shaped by physical contact with the slopes and surfaces of arms and breasts.

Jacquetta Hawkes saw the Downs as 'muscular hills', although she noted a paradox: that these powerful forms are made from of easily-eroded chalk. 'It would seem', she wrote, 'that instead of having been worn away particle after particle by water and wind some sculptor had succeeded in achieving that sense of force thrusting from within.'[76] You can imagine those muscles poised here under the sward, a word that derives from the Old English for rind or skin, suggesting that the turf is the 'skin' of the earth. There is a feeling of latent energy under the grass.

The South Downs have been repeatedly compared to the body by writers on Sussex. This is why coming to their sudden termination here at the cliff edge can seem so shocking. There is a break here that exposes the white bones of the hills to the salt wind and cold sea.

# Mirrors

Bill Brandt must have identified particularly with these cliffs because he chose this stark setting in 1966 for a self-portrait. In the image he is shot dramatically from below, dressed in black like a priest. His head is outlined in shadow against the white clouds and behind him stands the rough grey wall of the cliffs. However, this is not a direct self-portrait, it is a photograph of a mirror, propped up on the beach and held in place by a chalk stone. Brandt is both framed and reflected by the landscape.

At the sea's edge you catch only glimpses of yourself in the water, before each wave breaks it up. Suggestions of facial features in the shadows of the rocks are quickly dispelled. There is a painting of a sea cliff by August Strindberg that is said to hide his portrait, though it is only when imagined upside down that the rock face resembles his distinctive profile.[77] The blank chalk surfaces of the cliffs cannot really show us ourselves. Instead this succession of walls seems to echo and magnify our silent thoughts.

Along the coast at Dover, famous faces have been projected onto the White Cliffs by advertisers. Giant images of footballers, for example, appeared there in 1998, on the eve of the World Cup Finals. In 2012 David Beckham made a return appearance at the other end of his career, posing this time in a pair of underpants to promote his clothing line. Of course advertisers are attracted to the cliffs at Dover because of their symbolism and place in the national psyche. The Seven Sisters are different and have remained, as far as I know, untarnished by any advertisements.

# Illusions

Centuries before cliffs were turned by advertisers into billboards, they were used as a lure for ships. Lights were attached to cattle and sailors would mistake them for distant boats on a non-existent horizon. The ships ran aground and their cargo was looted. This history of deception continued in the smuggling era, when the cliffs were regularly patrolled by coastguards. The paths they marked with lumps of chalk to be visible at night could easily be moved. It is recorded that one night in 1750, an exciseman called Thomas Fletcher plunged to his death, deceived by a path the smugglers had re-built so that it took him over the edge of the cliff.[78]

These high walls of solid rock were a difficult place to conceal anything, but smugglers were ingenious. A fraternity near Beachy Head disguised themselves as shepherds. Whilst pretending to collect seabirds' eggs, they secretly managed to excavate an entire platform from which they were subsequently able to haul up tubs of contraband spirit.[79]

For a time, during the Second World War, wooden decoy Spitfires were used at nearby Friston airbase, whilst the Cuckmere valley was lit at night to simulate the appearance of Newhaven and lure the German bombers off course.[80] Thanks to the inter-War efforts at conservation, this phantom town is the nearest the landscape came to being built over. Nevertheless, we still walk here on a kind of natural stage where even the buildings and river can be repositioned. These days the cliffs are increasingly used by directors wanting a stand-in for the White Cliffs of Dover, free of any modern development.

# Wrapped Coast

In 1969 the land artists Christo and Jeanne-Claude created one of their best known early works, *Wrapped Coast*. Using 90,000 square meters of erosion-control fabric and 56 kilometres of polypropylene rope, they transformed a craggy shoreline south of Sydney into something that more closely resembled a chalk cliffscape.

How would this fake coastal feature have changed people's experiences of being there? For some it must have de-familiarised a place they had known for years. Perhaps in covering over the natural backdrop to their experiences it brought old memories back into focus. For others, with no prior knowledge of that coastline, the reality of the landscape could only be imagined, hidden under a vast dust sheet.

*Wrapped Coast* had its own unique qualities, moving with the wind, creating a cliff surface in constant motion. But it also obscured and smoothed over the irregularities of real earth and rock. Something like this happens when we view cliffs at a distance, as a landscape composed of shapes and simple colours. This might seem suspect: standing on a height to enjoy a panoramic view, unable to perceive the particularities of the place and reducing it to a surface over which the eye can travel at will. Here though, the walk will eventually take you down from the all-encompassing cliff tops. At sea level the true complexity of things comes back into focus, the qualities of each pebble, the patterns on the shoreline made by each individual wave.

# Harmonies

The Downs here resemble breakers hanging suspended over the beach. They are waves, in a sense, having slowly risen with the uplifting of the Alps. On their crests you are too high up to feel the breeze that catches spray off the real waves below, but it reaches you eventually, brushing through clumps of knapweed and clover, setting in motion hundreds of daisies and stirring up currents in the grass. H. J. Massingham thought the Downs conveyed the *illusion* of movement, 'free, unlike the sea, of unrest.'[81] But you are aware here that even the cropped grass is never still.

A butterfly on the path, an Adonis Blue I think, has white-flecked wings that resemble the surface of the sea. There are small correspondences like this everywhere, even though the landscape seems composed into distinct regions of land, sea and air. Another local species, the Chalkhill Blue, is, as its name suggests, a living emblem of the Downs. Each grey wing rises from its pale blue body to an earth-brown apex, with a delicate fringe like sunlit grass on the summit of the cliffs.

Daisies, cowslips, birds-foot trefoil and lady's bedstraw reflect the colours of sunshine and chalk. But there are contrasts here too, with clusters of pink and purple and blue: thrift, centaury, eyebright, viper's bugloss. At different times of the year you will see other flowers but the same colours repeat themselves, from the cowslips and buttercups, dog violets and early purple orchids of spring, to the thyme and thistles still visible in autumn, and the early flowering of furze in December.

The Seven Sisters appear unchanged by the seasons. Perhaps the migratory birds look out for their distinctive forms when they arrive from the south, then register them again on their return journey.[82] The whiteness of the cliffs can be glimpsed on the underside of kittiwakes and herring gulls as they wheel overhead. The waves, too, take on the colour of chalk at the limit of their reach, before disappearing into the shingle. Only the cliffs seem essentially, permanently white, gaining in brilliance and fading into pale shadow with the passage of the sun.

# Another Plane of Thought

The colour harmonies visible at widely different scales along the Seven Sisters are a temptation to ignore anything that fails to conform. How to accommodate, for example, the extraordinary burnet moths, with their shiny black wings covered in bright red spots? They look exotic but are as common here as the clumps of clover they alight upon.

To register nothing on this walk but a succession of attractive patterns and arrangements of colour would be a superficial experience, but quite how much knowledge is necessary for a serious appreciation of our surroundings is not easy to say. Few visitors bring a deep scientific understanding of the local ecosystem. A walk may be enriched with a guide to Downland flowers and a pair of binoculars to watch the seabirds, but sometimes, surely, it is good to leave these things at home.

An understanding of the processes that shaped an environment may only get us so far. As the mathematical biologist D'Arcy Wentworth Thompson wrote in his influential book *Growth and Form* (1917), it cannot fully explain to us how we feel about certain landscapes.

> The waves of the sea, the little ripples on the shore, the sweeping curve of the sandy bay between the headlands, the outline of the hills, the shape of the clouds, all these are so many riddles of form, so many problems of morphology, and all of them the physicist can more or less easily read and adequately solve: solving them by reference to antecedent phenomena, in the material system of mechanical forces to which they belong, and to which we interpret them as being due. They have also, doubtless, their immanent teleological significance; but it is on another plane of thought from the physicists that we contemplate their intrinsic harmony and perfection, and 'see that they are good.'[83]

# Significant Form

The sinusoidal profile of the cliff tops, the horizontal sea, the curvature of the river, the slopes of the Downs. All of these could be elements of an aesthetic equation, solvable mathematically by clever readers of *The Ladies' Diary*. An explanation for the beauty of the Seven Sisters seems graspable if we could only simplify it down to a question of geometry.

The landscape here seems arranged as if to demonstrate the doctrine of 'significant form' put forward by the Bloomsbury art critic Clive Bell, who lived nearby at Charleston. 'Who,' he asked, 'has not, once at least in his life, had a sudden vision of landscape as pure form? In that moment has he not won from material beauty a thrill indistinguishable from that which art gives?'[84]

When Bell suggests that it is possible to see a landscape free of 'all that it may have acquired from its commerce with human beings, from all its significance as a means', he assumes a reader willing to ignore the flux and noise of the lived environment. At the Seven Sisters this seems easy to do. You can gaze on a landscape that has no obvious 'significance as a means', until you reflect that the Seven Sisters Country Park is actively managed as a means of providing us with aesthetic pleasure.

And yet, no matter how we alter the character of this place, sometimes protecting it, sometimes polluting it, the fundamentals remain: the grass, the rocks, the water and the air. They may not really be pure and distinct from each other, but we can still experience them as essential natural forms. What Clive Bell wanted was to perceive, shorn of its associations, 'the thing itself'. Seeing significant form was for him a means of catching, fleetingly, a sense of ultimate reality.

# Essentials

In 1936 H. J. Massingham wrote that 'the frequenter of downlands is occupied with essentials; with structure, with forms and with textures.' There is no blurring of things, no confusion of line. 'Aloft, he breathes an air that tunes him to the grand, archaic, naked forms of things.'[85] Massingham thought it 'inconceivable that the Downs could be enjoyed or convey something of their spirit except for men and women, together or alone, whose mental life is personal and judgement their own.'[86] The masses, he thought, would head for the beaches at Brighton or Eastbourne.

The worry surfaces again that this walk is a means of climbing above the realities of everyday life. In cities now, the rich and super-rich live at the summit of cliff-like high-rise apartment blocks. For Massingham the high slopes of the Downs were a refuge from the Machine Age. Today the long views and open spaces feel like an escape from the digital world. It might be argued that this is exactly the kind of landscape that could have been rendered on a computer, with its flat sky, vivid green grass, smooth slopes and fractal cliffs. It doesn't feel like this now though, walking again into the wind on the brow of the cliffs.

Of course, everything here has been highly managed, from the cut diverting water from the Cuckmere's meanders to the concrete reinforcement walls preventing erosion of the cliffs. But this does not mean it is only possible to have artificial experiences here. Nor, it seems to me, is it less enlightening to visit the Seven Sisters than places more obviously undergoing transformation from the rapid economic and social changes we are all experiencing. Debates over the future of the cliffs and river, as sea levels rise, mark this out as a true twenty-first century landscape. It is precisely the tension between change and preservation that makes the experiences we have here so poignant.

# Desire Paths

Although the Seven Sisters are now much better known than they were when Massingham was writing, they are not yet overcrowded with visitors. The Seven Sisters Country Park website nevertheless states that 'to help manage the huge numbers of people who visit the Park each year, it is divided into two zones: the activity zone and the remote zone.' These zones continue to make a distinction between different ways of appreciating the outdoors. Walking the cliff tops I am in the 'remote zone', where cycling and kite flying is discouraged. Here, it seems, we are being asked to slow down and concentrate on the experience of landscape.

We are not yet in the future Marek Kohn has imagined, where visitors will no longer be allowed to ramble at will around Cuckmere Haven, but are tracked by GPS and fined if they stray from the path.[87] There are no restrictions now on where exactly I place my steps. Paths over the turf emerge as worn patches and exposed areas of chalk. They are 'desire paths' revealing the preferences of those walkers that have preceded me, although roughly how old they are I do not know.

Haven Brow has a complex pattern of paths. Some people have climbed straight over the summit to get down to the river, some have headed instead to the cliff edge, and some have started on the direct route and been seduced halfway by the thought of the sea. At various places the path meanders down the sloping turf, creating forms that echo the curves of the River Cuckmere. Water would head straight down these slopes but when it gets too steep walkers prefer to reduce the gradient. Adult walkers that is; children simply run to the bottom, as fast as young streams.

# Young Pebbles

There is a childlike quality to pebbles. They were seen in this way by the French poet Francis Ponge, released from the bedrock but not yet ground down to featureless gravel, 'each pebble lies on a heap of its ancient and future forms.' They may be a dull grey but they shine when water passes over them. Then, as Ponge observed, 'for a moment, the exterior of the pebble resembles its interior: its whole body is infused with the glow of youth.'[88]

I have been coming to the Seven Sisters for forty years, first as a child, more recently with my own children. Over that time I can remember walks in moods of optimism, sadness and simple, quiet contentment. The line of the cliffs could represent the ups and downs of a lifetime: from Went Hill to Haven Brow, Shakespeare's Seven Ages of Man. The river too is a metaphor for time. The Cuckmere flows relatively quickly from youth and maturity to old age before reaching the sea.

That we look on landscapes with wiser, sadder eyes as we get older is an idea almost too obvious to state. Wordsworth recalled his younger self responding directly to colours and forms, before he 'learned / To look on nature, not as in the hour / Of thoughtless youth, but hearing oftentimes / The still, sad music of humanity.'[89] He wrote these lines looking at old abbey walls whose history could be read in their ruination. The Seven Sisters are weathered and worn, yet they can seem to stand outside human time. Their blank surfaces face the tides that come and go as the sea constantly renews itself.

The Cuckmere passes between the cliffs, flowing onto the beach over remnants of stones originally washed here by meltwater from the Ice Age glaciers. Its cold, fresh water rejuvenates the pebbles and then disappears into the waves.

# Sea Interludes

The sea below me surges gently in and rattles back through the shingle. On a calm day like this the waves have the slow rhythm of sleep. They are unthreatening, undramatic. Perhaps they are monotonous – Claude Debussy, correcting the proofs of *La Mer* near here at Eastbourne's Grand Hotel, observed that 'the sea unfurls itself with an utterly British correctness'.[90]

Debussy did not see value in trying to find musical equivalents for distinct elements in nature. He thought Beethoven's *Pastoral Symphony* had more beauty than a landscape 'because there is no attempt at direct imitation, but rather at capturing the *invisible* sentiments of nature. Does one render the mystery of the forest by recording the height of the trees? It is more a process where the limitless depths of the forest give free reign to the imagination.'[91]

Yet if music cannot represent the sensory experience of a particular place directly, the composer can still convey something of its essential character. Gavin Bryars has said that his composition, *The South Downs,* was inspired by the view from Birling Gap, between the Seven Sisters and Beachy Head.[92] Its mournful waves of cello may not describe the cliffs in any obvious way, but I wonder how differently it would sound if Bryars had conceived it inland, where the South Downs are not exposed to the sea.

Another composer, Frank Bridge, loved this shoreline. Benjamin Britten used to visit him at Friston and they would take long walks by Beachy Head, go 'prawning', and play tennis.[93] Perhaps a few memories of the sounds here flowed into the *Sea Interludes* in Britten's *Peter Grimes.*[94] Memories of other coasts on other days shape all our encounters with the sea. The sounds of the surf on the stones today are a quiet echo of all the waves I have ever heard.

# The Sound of the Wind

'To get the true spirit of the Sussex Downs, you must become a lover of the wind'.[95] This was the advice of the Reverend Tickner Edwardes, master bee-keeper, early film-maker, writer of novels and author of the first book on hitch-hiking. The Downs, he said, 'are as a strung harp, that will yield no music save to the touch of one gargantuan player.'

If the Downs are a giant Aeolian harp, what of the Seven Sisters? Their undulant profile is suggestive of a musical phrase or the outline of a guitar in the Cubist collages that influenced John Piper. At Fingal's Cave, where Felix Mendelssohn was inspired to write his *Hebrides Overture*, the basalt columns and echoing vault in the rock face had a reputation as a kind of natural organ. There are no real cavities here in which the sea air can resonate. Instead the chalk cliffs mark the point at which the breath of the sea is channelled into the slopes of the hills.

As you walk over these slopes the noise from the sea rises and falls. Each of the Seven Sisters is different but their sounds resemble each other. Descending from peak to trough, the noise of wind and waves recedes to an almost inaudible susurrus. There are bees and insects, the sheep further inland, the distant drone of a light aircraft. Somewhere far above, the sound of a skylark.

# Silent cliffs

That idea of 'one gargantuan player' making music on the Downs reminds me of a story Rabelais tells about Pantagruel, son of the giant Gargantua.[96] Pantagruel questions the captain of a ship about voices they can hear coming to them from across the sea. The captain says that they are the sounds of a battle that had taken place in these waters the previous winter. The melting ice was now releasing frozen sounds into the air. Soldiers had died but their voices were preserved to emerge only later, like fossils exposed by a rock fall.

Legends of words frozen in the air go back at least to Plutarch and include a story told by Joseph Addison of travellers struck dumb by the extreme cold. When the air began to thaw, Addison writes, 'I soon after felt a breeze of whispers rushing by my ear; for those being of a soft and gentle substance, immediately liquefied in the warm wind that blew across our cabin.'[97] Soon, however, he was assailed by a cacophony of all the words that had been silenced over the course of the previous weeks.

If we long today for a break from noise and chatter, the silent cliffs offer a welcome relief. I imagine them absorbing sound like thick snow. Here on their summit you can barely make out the noise of the sea, just a quiet breathing. Swinburne, in his poem 'On the Downs', describes a place that sounds like this one.

> … on the lip's edge of the down,
> Here where the bent-grass burns to brown
>     In the dry sea-wind, and the heath
> Crawls to the cliff-side and looks down,
>     I watch, and hear beneath
>         The low tide breathe.[98]

# Climbing the Chalk

When Algernon Charles Swinburne was seventeen, frustrated at being prevented from volunteering for the army, he set out to prove himself by scaling a chalk cliff. Having taken a souse in the sea to steady his nerves, he had a startling thought. 'How easy it would be to climb the whole face of the cliff naked – or at least how much more sure one would feel of being able to do it – if one did not mind mere scratches or bruises; but to that prehistoric sort of proceeding there were obviously other objections than the atmosphere of midwinter. So I dressed and went straight at it.'[20]

Eventually he neared the summit where the cliff jutted out above him. Here even a seagull would not have been able to progress further without using its wings, and so he was forced to descend. But, reluctant to give in, he began climbing again using a different route. On his way up this time he disturbed a flock of gulls, whose music reminded him of the Eton Chapel organ. 'I was a little higher, quite near the top or well within hail of it, when I thought how queer it would be if my very scanty foothold gave way; and at that very minute it did.' Swinging by his hands for a moment he threw his feet towards a projection of rock and managed to get his breath before crawling up the final feet to the cliff top.

At the summit he lay exhausted, musing on how easy it would be to roll back over the edge and into the sea. Recalled to consciousness by a curious sheep, he returned home to find everyone out looking for him and his mother worried that he might try it again. 'Of course not — where could be the fun?' he assured her, 'I only wanted to do it because nobody thought it could.'

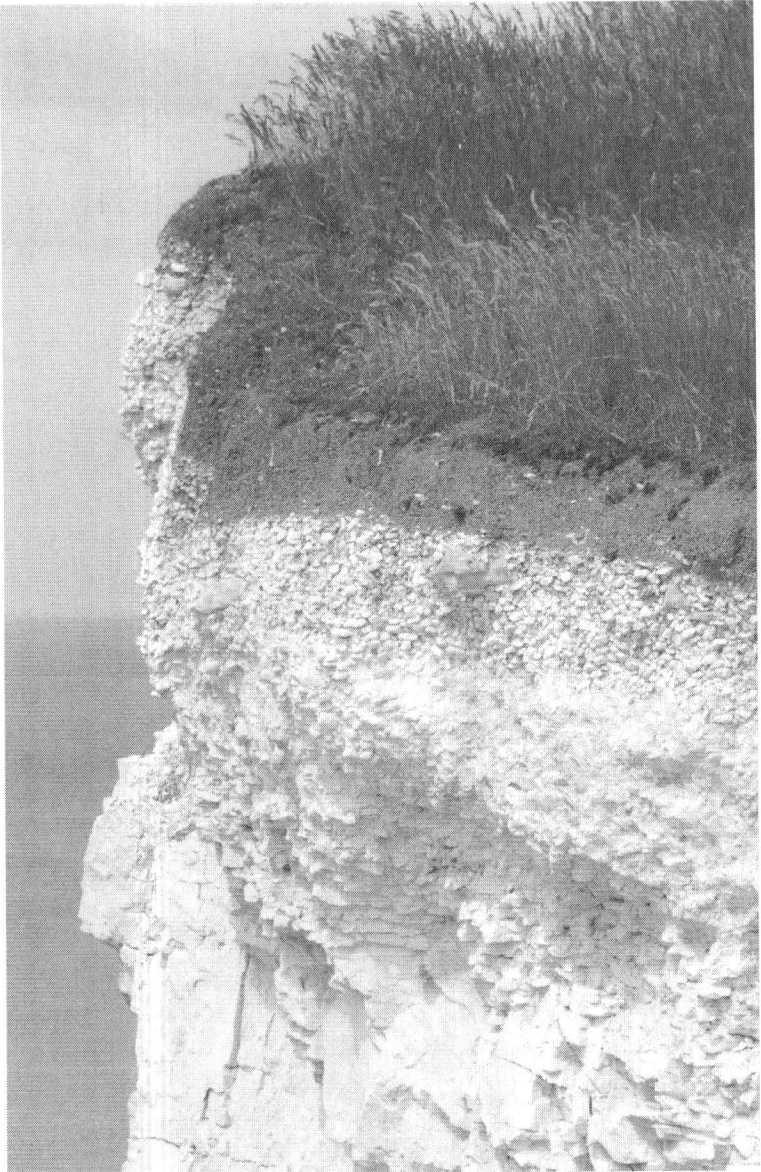

# Summit of Grass

The closest I will ever get to scaling the Seven Sisters is puffing up the steep path that leads to the summit of Haven Brow. It is easy though to see why the challenge of their sheer surfaces would be a strong draw for climbers. In their unadulterated whiteness the cliffs look as if no foot can ever have touched them. The British Mountaineering Council advise that the Seven Sisters can be climbed using 'ice techniques'. At close quarters, they must appear like high altitude cliffs of ice.

An ascent of these sea cliffs would allow a climber to feel they had reached another plane. On a mountain, the end point is a cold pinnacle or cluster of windswept rocks, where the only way is down. Cliffs take the climber from stony ground at sea level to a summit of soft grass and gentle paths. On reaching the top, a vertical world suddenly becomes horizontal. The climber becomes a walker, free to set off in any direction they choose.

We live a good part of our lives separated from the blue sky by layers of dull whiteness. Perhaps a cliff climb enacts the desire to get up into the clouds and emerge beyond them into the clear air. At the summit here you would be able to gaze over the Cuckmere Valley and beyond, to the distant blue Weald. The feeling would be similar to the relief felt by a tired traveller on finally glimpsing the longed-for sea. Or you could lie back on the clifftop and rest, opening your eyes occasionally to watch seabirds climb on the wind.

# Insensate Folly

Edward Whymper, a famous figure from the nineteenth century golden age of alpinism, begins his book *Scrambles Amongst the Alps* with an engraving not of mountain peaks but of tall white cliffs seen from the sea. 'As we steamed out into the Channel, Beachy Head came into view, and recalled a scramble of many years ago. With the impudence of ignorance, my brother and I, schoolboys both, had tried to scale that great chalk cliff ... Since then we have been often in dangers of different kinds, but never have we more nearly broken our necks than upon that occasion.'[100] The cliffs were a foretaste of the Alps and a testing ground for the young climber.

'Insensate folly takes various forms. One of the most dangerous is that of attempting to climb chalk cliffs on the southern coast.'[101] This was the *Eastbourne Gazette's* view of a climb undertaken by the eighteen year old Aleister Crowley and his cousin in 1894. Writing his own account in the *Scottish Mountaineering Journal*, Crowley warned climbers not to attempt such a climb on wet and windy days. 'On the former, the soddened chalk is slippery and dangerous, and too unpleasant in fact to be indulged in by the most enthusiastic. Dry windy days, on the other hand, when chalk particles, varying from fine dust to large nuggets, are being driven about, are fatal to the eyes, which may be bloodshot and sore for days afterwards.' However, the future magus and prophet of his own religion advised climbers to go 'with true worship, undaunted, and your reward shall be joy unspeakable in the glorious divinity of sun-glistening altitude and towering whiteness.'

In Crowley's description it is as if the mountaineer has realised the dream of an ascent into the clouds.

# To Cast One's Eyes So Low

In *King Lear*, Edgar leads his blinded father, Gloucester, to the summit of the cliff at Dover:

Come on, sir; here's the place: stand still. How fearful
And dizzy 'tis, to cast one's eyes so low!
The crows and choughs that wing the midway air
Show scarce so gross as beetles: half way down
Hangs one that gathers samphire, dreadful trade!
Methinks he seems no bigger than his head:
The fishermen, that walk upon the beach,
Appear like mice; and yond tall anchoring bark,
Diminish'd to her cock; her cock, a buoy
Almost too small for sight: the murmuring surge,
That on the unnumber'd idle pebbles chafes,
Cannot be heard so high. I'll look no more;
Lest my brain turn, and the deficient sight
Topple down headlong.[102]

This dizziness felt by Edgar is acrophobia, the fear of heights, from the Greek root 'acron'. Psychologists have investigated acrophobia in babies using an abstract 'visual cliff' drawn on a sheet of plexiglass suspended four feet above the ground. Most children, feeling the transparent but solid floor beneath them, ignore the visual cliff, but some are more hesitant or refuse to crawl at all. The cliff experiment has been used to test depth perception in animals: rats, who do not rely on visual clues ignore it, whereas cats are very reluctant to stray from the top of the cliff.

Gloucester may have lost his sight but Edgar's vision seems to have been heightened by the danger of that fearful vantage point. His description of the view is as detailed as a Flemish painting. On a cliff path all our senses feel more alert. Unsurprising then, that here we are also in a heightened state of receptiveness to the aesthetic qualities of everything we encounter.

# Fear of Heights

In an essay Joseph Addison published in 1709, he recalled having once been quartered near Dover with the army, where he

> 'fell in love with an agreeable young woman, of a good family in those parts, and had the satisfaction of seeing my addresses kindly received. … We were in a calm evening diverting ourselves upon the top of the cliff with the prospect of the sea, and trifling away the time in such little fondnesses as are most ridiculous to people in business, and most agreeable to those in love. In the midst of these our innocent endearments, she snatched a paper of verses out of my hand, and ran away with them. I was following her, when on a sudden the ground, though at a considerable distance from the verge of the precipice, sank under her, and threw her down from so prodigious a height upon such a range of rocks, as would have dashed her into ten thousand pieces, had her body been made of adamant.'[103]

It was at this moment that Addison woke up and realised he had been dreaming.

The memory of this dream was so powerful that Addison said he could 'never read the description of Dover Cliff in Shakespeare's tragedy of *King Lear*, without a fresh sense of my escape'. Perhaps subconsciously Addison's confidence in his writing, snatched away by the young woman, was no stronger than the cliff in his nightmare. It is a feeling that can accompany any cherished project or creative endeavour, where the path in places skirts close to the edge of failure. Rather than look down at the rocks and surging water, it is easier to keep on walking, conscious of the sea only as a calm blue expanse in the distance.

# Soaring Flight

Herring gulls appear from beneath the cliff edge and rise above me, riding thermals that take them well beyond the limits of the land.

Watching the flight of birds I reflect on the way they draw attention to the sky's great extent, and emptiness. They call to mind the artist Peter Lanyon, who, like Swinburne before him, identified with the seagulls he saw at the sea's edge. Lanyon spoke of choosing to paint a cliff as it would be experienced by a bird, in abstract strokes like currents of air. In a beautiful phrase, he described the flight paths of the gulls, 'moulding the space between the rock and shore'.[104] Thought of in this way, the sky has its own weight and form, felt by the birds: a complex mobile structure impossible for us to perceive and experience without taking to the air. This is what Lanyon did, training to become a glider pilot, so that like the cliff climbers he could test his own limits at the edge of the land. He could also feel a freedom up there in the sky that was impossible to contain on a canvass.

As a child I was fascinated by the hang gliders at Devil's Dyke, drifting out over the scarp slope of the Downs near our home on the edge of Brighton. Watching them take off, it looked as if they were able to fly simply by stepping off the hill and resting on the wind that surged over the grass. Nowadays there are paragliders who seem even more at home in the air, filling the spectator with a feeling of physical lightness.

In his book on the Downs, W. H. Hudson imagined lifting great heron-like wings and taking flight from their summit. 'Here are no inviting woods and mysterious green shades that ask to be explored: they stand naked to the sky, and on them the mind becomes more aerial, less conscious of gravity and a too solid body.'[105]

# Aerial Dreams

Wondering whether anyone had tried to glide from the summit of the Seven Sisters, I came upon a set of black and white photographs taken in 1978, documenting a flight from Seaford Head. The glider could well have been one of those I had watched with my parents at Devil's Dyke. In one of these photographs he is seen from behind, looking out to a misty sunlit sea like a figure in a Romantic painting. There is a cliff edge warning sign nearby, but he stands poised under his glider ready to fly. In the next image he is off, circling in front of the chalk face, gradually losing height. After a short sequence of these photographs we see him hit the waves far below, seemingly lost to view, like Icarus. But the final images show him unharmed down among the surf and chalk boulders, retrieving his glider from the water.[106]

There are limits to how far a glider's wings can take us. The aerial dreams these hills and cliffs inspire can only truly be realised in stories. There is a legend that King Solomon was borne by the winds on a square of green silk stretching sixty miles, almost as wide as the Downs. I imagine the grass here gently sliding from its bed of chalk and ascending into the sky, an airborne island, floating slowly above the water and sailing eventually out over the ocean.

When I was growing up the film *Chitty Chitty Bang Bang* was televised every Christmas holiday. The high point was that miraculous moment when a car is transformed into a flying machine. Caractacus Potts, hotly in pursuit of Baron von Bomburst of Vulgaria's zeppelin, is too busy looking up at the sky to notice that he is veering off a Downland track and heading up a grass incline. A glimpse of the Seven Sisters indicates that there will be nothing but sea beyond the brow of the slope. As they drive over the edge, the cliff face rushes past behind them, but just before they hit the water, the car extends her wings and they soar back up and away.

# The Sun and the Sky

The sun is hot now and the sky, misty at the horizon, is almost clear of clouds above me. Over the course of a walk, it has changed character as the clouds have formed and almost dispersed. The lucent, pale blue I saw earlier has become a colour that I cannot describe without using words like azure or sapphire. The sky has the purity we imagine when we think of polished gems, but none of their hardness.

In one of his extraordinary books on the elemental imagination, *Air and Dreams*, the French philosopher Gaston Bachelard described the different ways that poets have imagined the sky. There have been those 'who see in an immobile sky a flowing liquid that comes to life with the smallest cloud', those who 'experience the blue sky as though it were an enormous flame', those who 'contemplate the sky as if it were a solidified blue, a pointed vault' and those who 'truly participate in the aerial nature of celestial blue.'[107] Today the sky high above me is a celestial blue and I can imagine the stars that will be visible when the sun goes down, and the moon, which even now is leading the tide in.

I look down over the beach to see if the river channel is still fordable. I will have to return that way soon, but would rather stay aloft for a while, suspended on the frozen air of the cliffs with these long views in every direction. Reclining on the turf, I feel the heat of the sun and my eyes rest on nothing but blue emptiness and a few wisps of cloud, miles above me.

# Butterfly at Rest

There is a passage in W. H. Hudson's book that recalls a long ramble over these hills, encountering nobody until he neared the sea.

> On approaching a coastguard station I all at once came upon some children lying on the grass on the slope of a down. There were five of them, scattered about, all lying on their backs, their arms stretched crossways, straight out, their hands open. It looked as if they had instinctively spread themselves out, just as a butterfly at rest opens wide its wings to catch the beams. The hot sun shone full on their fresh young faces; and though wide awake they lay perfectly still as I came up and walked slowly past them, looking from upturned face to face, each expressing perfect contentment.[108]

I wonder what became of those children. Perhaps they lived near here and saw the landscape preserved from developers, fortified against invasion and then grow increasingly popular with Sunday walkers and ramblers down from London. Perhaps they moved away and returned, as I do, on summer days, feeling again the tug of the sea, glimpsed first through a dip in the Downs and then visible in its entirety from the brow of the cliff, here at the edge of the land.

I try to imagine how many more people will be able to sit here before this section of chalk crumbles away. On a still, hot day like this it is hard to envisage anything changing, even though three hundred feet below me the river has set itself a new course. I stand up and enjoy for a minute the feel of the light salt wind. Then I turn and make my way down towards the beach where I can hear voices and laughter and, as I get closer, the quiet breath of the low tide. Behind me the grass slopes steeply up towards the sky where the gulls slowly climb and descend.

# Acknowledgements

I should like to thank Lisa, Lorcan and Torin for their company on the cliffs. For encouragement and specific suggestions I am grateful to Robert Macfarlane, Gareth Evans, Kathryn Yusoff, James Attlee, Roman Krznaric, Louise Ray, Ian Rawes, Ken and Larraine Worpole, and all the readers of *Some Landscapes*. This book is for my parents who continue to walk this stretch of coast and who introduced me to the Seven Sisters.

# Endnotes

[1] 'Beauty is felt as the sudden contact with an aspect of reality that one has not known before; it is the antithesis of the acquired taste for certain landscapes or the warm feeling for places that one knows well.' Tuan, Yi-Fu, *Topophilia: A study of Environmental Perception, Attitudes and Values* (Englewood Cliffs: Prentice-Hall, 1974) p. 94

[2] Tolkien, J. R. R., *Unfinished Tales* (London: George Allen & Unwin, 1980) p. 25

[3] Xenophon, *The Expedition of Cyrus*, trans. Robin Waterfield (Oxford: OUP, 2005) p. 101

[4] Proust, Marcel, *Pleasures and Days*, trans. Andrew Brown (London: Hesperus, 2004) p. 147

[5] Proust, Marcel, *In Search of Lost Time, Volume 4: Sodom and Gomorrah*, trans. C. K. Scott Moncrieff & Terence Kilmartin, revised by D. J. Enright (London: Vintage, 1996) p. 211

[6] These littoral communities appear, for example, in a poem which shares Proust's conceit, written in the seventeenth century by Margaret Cavendish: 'Similizing the Sea to Meadowes, and Pastures, the Marriners to Shepheards, the Mast to a May-pole, Fishes to Beasts'. Walking here now I never see a farmer or a sailor.

[7] See http://www.theguardian.com/business/2014/may/30/rolls-royce-remote-controlled-cargo-ships

[8] Since writing this, construction of the windfarm has begun, but the original plans were scaled down.

[9] Maleuvre, Didier, *The Horizon* (Berkeley & Los Angeles: University of California Press, 2011) p. xiii

[10] Look in a straight line from the top of the Seven Sisters and you will be facing Cabourg, the inspiration for Proust's Balbec.

[11] Pastoureau, Michel, *Blue: The History of a Color*, trans. Markus I. Cruse (Princeton & Oxford: Princeton University Press, 2001) p. 163

[12] Maleuvre, Didier, *The Horizon* p. 3

[13] The idea that a shoreline could represent the edge of an artwork was explored by the land artists Christo and Jeanne-Claude, who encircled a string of islands in bright plastic, turning them into a series of sculptures.

[14] In *Richard II Act 2 Scene 1:* 'This precious stone set in the silver sea, / Which serves it in the office of a wall, / Or as a moat defensive to a house, / Against the envy of less happier lands…'

[15] Derrida, Jacques, *The Truth in Painting*, trans. Geoff Bennington and Ian McLeod, (Chicago & London: University of Chicago Press, 1987) pp. 57-60

[16] Jefferies, Richard, *Nature Near London* (London: Collins, 2012) p. 198

[17] Hudson, W. H., *Nature in Downland and An Old Thorn* (London and Toronto: J. M. Dent, 1932) p. 35

[18] Quoted in *The South Downs* by 'The Tramp', a book published by the London, Brighton & South Coast Railway (no date but circa 1910)

[19] Its branches resemble the spokes of a wind-rose, a graph meteorologists use to plot the frequency of winds from each point of the compass.

[20] Jefferies, Richard, *Nature Near London* p. 197

[21] Burton, Robert, *The Anatomy of Melancholy* (New York: The New York Review of Books, 2001) p. 61

[22] 'The Downs' in Bridges, Robert, *Robert Bridges: Poetry & Prose* (Oxford: Clarendon Press, 1955) p. 26

[23] Hardy, Thomas, *A Pair of Blue Eyes* (Oxford: OUP, 2005) p. 193

[24] Mason, Chr., 'Question 198' in Cha. Hutton ed., *The Diarian Miscellany* Vol. II (London: Robinson and Baldwin, 1775) p. 71

[25] The imposing memorial to Marx we are familiar with today was only erected in 1956. On its unveiling *The Manchester Guardian*'s correspondent wrote that 'although the colour is bilious and the inflated proportions are monstrous at close quarters, it is not without grandeur' (15 March 1956). When Marx died in 1883 his funeral had been attended by only eleven people.

[26] The National Trust's Robertson Memorials – see https://historicengland.org.uk/listing/the-list/list-entry/1438498

[27] The sketches of coastlines made in mariners' logs, which sometimes included ships to give a sense of scale, can be seen as a precursor of the marine painting genre - see Mack, John, *The Sea: A Cultural History* (London: Reaktion Books, 2011) p. 31

[28] Kohn, Marek, *Turned Out Nice: How the British Isles will Change as the World Heats Up* (London: Faber, 2010) p. 107

[29] Kohn, Marek, *Turned Out Nice* p. 105

[30] Gilbert, Richard, *Everyman's Sussex* (London: Robert Scott, 1927) p. 76

[31] Lyell, Charles, *Principles of Geology, Volume 1* (London: John Murray, 1830) p. 279

[32] Ingold, Tim, 'Landscape or Weather World?' in *Being Alive: Essays on Movement, Knowledge and Description* (London & New York: Routledge, 2011)

[33] Southam, Jem, *Rockfalls and Ponds* (Madrid: Fundación Telefónica, 2010) p. 16

[34] This image comes from Andrew Young's poem 'The Chalk-Cliff', in Andrew Young, *Selected Poems* (Manchester: Carcanet, 1998) p. 63

[35] See the Seven Sisters Country Park site, http://www.sevensisters.org.uk/page64.html

[36] Of the seven planted in 1902 to mark the coronation of Edward II only one survived the Great Storm of 1987. The six replacements installed in a special ceremony by a group of celebrities were destroyed by vandals. More have been planted.

[37] Corbin, Alain, *The Lure of the Sea*, trans. Jocelyn Phelps (Harmondsworth: Penguin, 1995) p. 122

[38] Smith, Charlotte, *The Poems of Charlotte Smith* (Oxford: OUP, 1993) p. 218

[39] Quoted in the *Sussex Express*, 16 May 2003

[40] Jefferies, Richard, *Nature Near London* p. 192

[41] Kipling, Rudyard, *Selected Poems* (London: Penguin, 1993) p. 108

[42] Henrietta Elizabeth Marshall's *Our Island Story: A Child's History of England* was published in 1905.

[43] Martin, Peter, *Ghost Music: Poetry and History of Seaford and the Cuckmere Valley* (Seaford: Seaford Arts, 2010) p. 37

[44] Waugh, Mary, *Smuggling in Kent & Sussex 1700-1840* (Newbury: Countryside Books, 1985) p. 111

[45] Smith, Charlotte, *The Poems of Charlotte Smith* p. 218

[46] Amos, Jonathan, 'Megaflood 'made Island Britain'' (2007) http://news.bbc.co.uk/1/hi/sci/tech/6904675.stm

[47] Smith, Charlotte, *The Poems of Charlotte Smith* p. 246

[48] Originally called *Our English Coasts*, it had been partly intended as a comment on the defenceless state of the country against a possible French invasion under Napoleon III. It was given the new title in 1855.

[49] Parris, Leslie ed., *The Pre-Raphaelites* (London: Tate Publishing, 1995) p. 108

[50] See http://www.eastbourneherald.co.uk/news/east-dean-attraction-set-to-close-after-the-summer-1-7472031

[51] Arnold, Matthew, 'Dover Beach' in George MacBeth ed. *Victorian Verse* (Harmondsworth: Penguin, 1986) p. 166

[52] Amos, Jonathan, 'Beer microbes live 553 days outside ISS' (2010) http://www.bbc.co.uk/news/science-environment-11039206

[53] Young, Andrew, *Selected Poems* (Manchester: Carcanet, 1998) p. 97

[54] Godfrey, John, *The New Shell Guides: Sussex* (London: Michael Joseph, 1990) p. 71

[55] Beckett, Arthur, *The Spirit of the Downs* (London: Methuen & Co., 1909) p. 248

[56] Martin, Peter, *Ghost Music: Poetry and History of Seaford and the Cuckmere Valley* p. 37

[57] Jonathan Danby became vicar in 1706 and 'with his own hands he hollowed out a room in the face of the cliff, well above the high-tide line, and constructed a sloping tunnel and steps to lead up to it from the beach. There, night after night when the seas ran high, the good parson hung a lamp outside his cave and waited within, sheltered in a side recess from the winds, to help any sailors who might be struggling to reach shore.' Mee, Arthur, *Sussex: The Garden by the Sea* (London: Hodder & Stoughton, 1937) p. 132

[58] Smith, Charlotte, *The Poems of Charlotte Smith* p. 245

[59] See Appleton, Jay, *The Experience of Landscape: Revised Edition* (New York: Wiley, 1996)

[60] Bourdillon, Francis William, 'Fair are the hills of Sussex', in C. F. Cook ed., *The Book of Sussex Verse* (Hove: Combridges, 1914) p. 161

[61] On the grass behind the Coastguard Cottages there is a simple flint memorial to a company of these Canadian soldiers. It is based on the testimony of a Home Guard farm worker who recalled warning the commanding officer that it was not safe to camp there. 'Two mornings later the Messerschmitts arrived. Just

as the sun was rising they came skimming over the water and up the valley. Around Alfriston they banked hard and came back. Bearing down on the tents they opened fire. Steam, soil and grass rose in front of them as bullets and bombs entered the ground. All the young men in the marquees and bell tents were killed. Their commanding officer who was shaving at the time in the middle coastguard cottage died instantly when a shell went through the wall that held his mirror'.

[62] Park, A., 'Written on the Sands Below Beachy Head', in C. F. Cook ed., *The Book of Sussex Verse* (Hove: Combridges, 1914) p. 161

[63] Kant, Immanuel, *The Critique of Judgement*, trans. James Creed Meredith (Oxford: OUP, 1952) p. 110

[64] This tradition is referred to, for example, in *The Faerie Queene* where Edmund Spenser writes that the island had no name 'Till that the venturous Mariner that way / Learning his ship from those white rocks to saue, / Which all along the Southerne sea-coast lay, / Threatning vnheedie wrecke and rash decay, / For safeties sake that same his sea-marke made, / And named it Albion.' (Book II, Canto X)

[65] Delaney, Paul, *Bill Brandt: A Life* (London: Jonathan Cape, 2004) p. 91

[66] Bishop, Elizabeth, *Complete Poems* (London: Chatto & Windus, 1991) p. 4

[67] Young, Andrew, *Selected Poems* p. 63

[68] Hawkes, Jacquetta, *A Land* (Harmondsworth: Pelican Books, 1959) p. 74

[69] Hawkes, Jacquetta, *A Land* p. 74

[70] Later the cement dust was found to have been killing the surrounding trees and much stricter regulations were imposed. Binyon, Helen, *Eric Ravilious: Memoir of an Artist* (Cambridge: The Lutterworth Press, 1983) p. 67

[71] The articles chosen compare the economic situations at the time in Britain ('The Unemployment Bill under Fire') and Germany ('Nazi Economics').

[72] Denvir, Bernard, *The Thames and Hudson Encyclopedia of Impressionism* (London: Thames & Hudson, 1990) p. 85

[73] Her diary records that 'there was a strong wind and a high sea and I posed for a nude – it was horribly uncomfortable and very cold and I was very bad tempered. But the tide was coming in so we had to be fairly quick & thank goodness.' Delaney, Paul, *Bill Brandt: A Life* (London: Jonathan Cape, 2004) p. 241

[74] The drawing is *Coastal Landscape* (1890-2) in the Galerie Jan Krugier, Geneva.

[75] It has been suggested that all landscapes resemble a loved or dreamed-of face – see Gilles Deleuze and Félix Guattari, *A Thousand Plateaus,* trans. Brian Massumi (London: Continuum, 2004) p. 191

[76] Hawkes, Jacquetta, *A Land* p. 198

[77] There are other examples. In 1909, for example, Giorgio De Chirico painted *Seascape with Rocks,* in which the line of the turf on top of a cliff is broken by a higher outcrop of rock which resembles a face looking out to sea. An alternative title is known which makes clear what this head on the cliff is: *The Sphinx.*

[78] Waugh, Mary, *Smuggling in Kent & Sussex 1700-1840* (Newbury: Countryside Books, 1985) p. 109

[79] Waugh, Mary, *Smuggling in Kent & Sussex 1700-1840* p. 115

[80] Longstaff-Tyrrell, Peter, *Operation Cuckmere Haven: An Investigation into military aspects of the Cuckmere Valley, East Sussex* (Polegate: Gote House Publishing, 1997) p. 37

[81] Massingham, H. J., *English Downland* (London: Batsford, 1949) p. 5

[82] In addition to using sight, birds can hear infrasound caused by movement in the wind and sea. They may also be able to smell a

landscape and feel it through changes in air temperature.  The sight of the white cliffs might therefore not be the dominant impression they have of the Seven Sisters.

[83] Thompson, D'Arcy Wentworth, *On Growth and Form: New Edition* (Cambridge: CUP, 1942) p. 10

[84] Bell, Clive, *Art* (Oxford: OUP, 1987) p. 53

[85] Massingham, H. J., *English Downland* p. 3

[86] Massingham, H. J., *English Downland* p. 8

[87] Kohn, Marek, *Turned Out Nice* p. 131

[88] Francis Ponge, 'The Pebble' in *Selected Poems*, trans. Margaret Guiton (London: Faber, 1994) p. 105

[89] Wordsworth, William, 'Lines Written a few Miles above Tintern Abbey' in *Selected Poems* (London: Penguin, 2004)  p. 61

[90] Nichols, Roger, *The Life of Debussy* (Cambridge: CUP, 1998) p. 117

[91] Trezise, Simon, *Debussy: La Mer* (Cambridge: CUP, 1994) p. 38

[92] See http://www.gavinbryars.com/work/composition/south-downs

[93] Marshall, E. M., *Music in the Landscape* (London: Robert Hale, 2011) p. 270

[94] The *Sea Interludes* have no specific references to the Suffolk setting of the opera's story.  Indeed on the BBC website you can actually listen to a recording of them whilst looking at a brooding Bill Brandt-style black and white photograph of the Seven Sisters, taken from Cuckmere Haven.  See http://www.bbc.co.uk/programmes/p01zfsx5

[95] Edwardes, Tickner, 'The True Sussex Highlander' in Margaret Goldsworthy, *Sussex Bedside Anthology* (Arundel: Arundel Press, 1950) p. 527

[96] Kahn, Douglas, *Noise Water Meat: A History of Sound in the Arts* (Cambridge, Mass. And London: The MIT Press, 1999) p. 205

[97] Addison, Joseph, *The Tatler* No. 254, 23rd November 1710

[98] Swinburne, Algernon Charles, *The Poems of Algernon Charles Swinburne in Six Volumes, Volume II: Songs Before Sunrise and Songs of Two Nations* (London: Chatto & Windus, 1905) p. 191

[99] Leith, Mrs. Disney, *The Boyhood of Algernon Charles Swinburne: Personal Recollections by His Cousin Mrs. Disney Leith* (London: Chatto & Windus, 1917) p. 14

[100] Gilchrist, Paul, 'Beyond the Brink: Beachy Head as a Climbing Landscape', *The International Journal of the History of Sport*, Volume 29, Issue 10, 2012, pp. 1383-1404

[101] Gilchrist, Paul, 'Beyond the Brink'

[102] Shakespeare, William, *King Lear* (London: The Arden Shakespeare, 1997) p. 327

[103] Addison, Joseph, *The Tatler*, No. 117, 7th January 1709

[104] Stephens, Chris, *Peter Lanyon: At the Edge of Landscape* (London: 21 Publishing, 2000) p. 36

[105] Hudson, W. H., *Nature in Downland* p. 27

[106] Liddard, Don, photographs of Peter Taylor's flight from the cliffs at Seaford in 1978, retrieved from https://www.flickr.com/photos/donliddard/tags/seaford/show/

[107] Bachelard, Gaston, *Air and Dreams*, trans. Edith R. Farrell (Dallas: The Dallas Institute Publications, 1988) p. 160

[108] Hudson, W. H., *Nature in Downland* p. 146

23483618R00055

Printed in Great Britain
by Amazon